U.S. ARMY GUARD
AND RESERVE

Studies in Defense Policy

STUDIES IN DEFENSE POLICY

U.S. ARMY GUARD AND RESERVE: RHETORIC, REALITIES, RISKS

Martin Binkin and
William W. Kaufmann

THE BROOKINGS INSTITUTION
Washington, D.C.

Library of Congress Cataloging-in-Publication Data

Binkin, Martin, 1928–
    U.S. Army Guard and Reserve: rhetoric, realities, risks /
Martin Binkin and William W. Kaufmann.
      p.   cm.—(Studies in defense policy)
    Includes index.
    ISBN 0-8157-0979-X (alk. paper)
    1. United States. Army—Reserves. 2. United States—
National Guard. I. Kaufmann, William W.
II. Title. III. Title: US Army Guard and
Reserve. IV. Series.
UA42.B48   1989   89-32428
355.3'7'0973—dc20   CIP

9 8 7 6 5 4 3 2 1

FOREWORD

SINCE THE early 1970s the U.S. Army has become increasingly dependent on its two reserve components, the Army National Guard and the Army Reserve. Today, in fact, citizen-soldiers bear unprecedented responsibilities for the nation's defense. The Army's reserve components are at their peak peacetime strength, accounting for more than half of the trained manpower in the Total Army, and they are assigned missions vital to both the warfighting capabilities and the sustainability of the Army. In a distinct break with the past, many reserve units are expected to deploy on as tight a timetable as active units. Indeed, nine of the eighteen active divisions could not fully deploy unless accompanied by the reserve combat brigades or battalions that fill out their structures. Moreover, the Army leans heavily on its reserve components to provide the tactical logistics support upon which the combat forces depend beyond the first week of a conflict.

In this study, Martin Binkin and William W. Kaufmann assess the implications of these trends. They ask whether the increased dependence on the Army's reserve forces is a sound strategy, and whether the planned mix of active and reserve forces would be able to fulfill, with reasonable confidence, the purposes for which they are designed. To answer those questions, the authors test the Army's current force structure against a range of contingencies under various assumptions about the combat power and effectiveness of reserve units. They conclude that even when the reserve components are credited with quite reasonable performance, considering deficiencies in the equipment and the amount of training they receive, the U.S. Army is not as ready as the rhetoric implies to execute the worldwide "strategic concept" involving multiple contingencies in Europe, Asia, and the Caribbean. The authors present the principal options available to decisionmakers to improve the status quo through changes in structure, orientation, and the strategic concept underlying the mix of active and reserve forces.

Martin Binkin, a senior fellow in the Brookings Foreign Policy Studies program, is author or coauthor of twelve previous books in the Brookings Studies in Defense Policy series. William Kaufmann is a consultant at Brookings, professor emeritus of the Massachusetts Institute of Technology, and a faculty member of the John F. Kennedy School of Government at Harvard University. The authors thank William K. Brehm and General Eugene C. Meyer for their thoughtful comments on the manuscript. They are also grateful to Brigadier General Raymond E. Bell, Jr. (U.S. Army Reserve), Kenneth J. Coffey, Richard B. Crossland, David A. Smith, Lewis Sorley, Harry J. Thie, John C. F. Tillson, and Wallace Earl Walker for helpful comments and to Brookings colleagues Richard K. Betts and Thomas L. McNaugher for their valuable suggestions. They are particularly indebted to John D. Steinbruner for his guidance and encouragement. The authors also thank Jeanette Morrison for editing the manuscript, Ann M. Ziegler and Susan L. Woollen for preparing it for production, Amy R. Waychoff, Shimon Avish, Vernon L. Kelley, and Daniel A. Lindley III for verifying its factual content, and Max Franke for preparing the index.

Brookings gratefully acknowledges the financial support for this study from the Ford Foundation and the John D. and Catherine T. MacArthur Foundation.

The views expressed in this study are those of the authors and should not be ascribed to the persons or organizations whose assistance is acknowledged, or to the trustees, officers, or other staff members of the Brookings Institution.

BRUCE K. MAC LAURY
President

April 1989
Washington, D.C.

CONTENTS

Tables

Figures

CHAPTER ONE

INTRODUCTION

In the nearly two decades since the Nixon administration decided to end conscription, America's military institution has undergone substantial changes. One of the most serious has been the expanded role given to the military's reserve components.

All the military services have reserve elements. The Army and the Air Force have two components each, a National Guard and a Reserve; the Navy and Marine Corps have one component each, the Naval Reserve and the Marine Corps Reserve. Under a so-called Total Force policy, the members of these units now shoulder unprecedented responsibilities for protecting the nation's security interests.

The effects have been most pronounced for the Army: in contrast to 1964, when reservists were 40 percent of trained Army manpower, by 1988 they made up about half of the total. According to projections made in 1988, moreover, the Army National Guard and Army Reserve were to continue to grow, while the size of the active Army was to be reduced.

Of greater importance than shifting force levels, though, are changes in the missions and responsibilities assigned to the reserve components. Traditionally, they were forces literally "held in reserve," with a cushion of time to complete mobilization and training. Today, many of the Army's reserve elements are expected to deploy along with the active forces, some with only a few days' notice and most of the remainder within weeks rather than months or years as in the past. Reserve units, both combat and support, would be among the earliest deployed in a range of conflicts—from fast-breaking limited contingencies to a major confrontation in Central Europe between NATO and the Warsaw Pact. According to present planning, for example, more than 40 percent of the Army forces deployed during the first thirty days of a European war would be reservists, and a sizable portion of the Army forces earmarked for the quick-reaction U.S. Central Command are reserves. As matters stand, few ground campaigns would be conducted without involving the Army's reserve components almost from the very beginning.

This unprecedented dependence on the reserves has been instituted with little public fanfare or debate, yet the consequences could be dramatic and far-reaching. A central issue is the effect that the "Total Army" policy will have on the nation's ability to protect its security interests. Of major concern is that the reserves are being counted as the equivalent of their active counterparts. Army reserve forces cost much less to maintain in peacetime, but they are also less trained, less equipped, and less ready than active forces. Also worrisome are the political factors that have complicated previous call-up, deployment, and demobilization decisions. These concerns persist despite initiatives taken under the Total Force policy to improve manning levels, training, and equipage.

Several questions need fresh and careful examination. Is the increased and earlier dependence on reserves a sound strategy, given their historical record and their inherent limitations? Will the planned mix of Army active and reserve forces—in conjunction with U.S. air and allied capabilities—be able to fulfill, with reasonable confidence, the purposes for which they are designed? If not, how can the structure and orientation of Army reserve forces be altered to raise that confidence, and at what cost?

Our analysis of these questions is organized as follows. Chapter 2 describes the organization, structure, and costs of the Army's reserve components, highlighting the unusually heavy responsibilities now being placed on them. How the Army arrived at the existing state of affairs is traced in chapter 3, which looks at the military, financial, and political factors that have shaped its current force posture.

Whether the Army reserves are up to their assigned tasks is explored in the next four chapters. The difficulties that have marked previous mobilizations are discussed in chapter 4, covering the historical experience with the use of Army reserve forces. The extent to which these problems have been fixed is the subject of chapter 5, which discusses the initiatives taken under the Total Force policy to improve the manning, training, and equipment status of the reserves and to make it easier for a president to use them. In chapter 6, the current capabilities of the Army reserves are discussed and their principal limitations examined. The Army's current force structure is tested in chapter 7 against a range of contingencies under various assumptions about warning time and the combat power and effectiveness of reserve units.

Against this background, the concluding chapter discusses the principal options available to decisionmakers to improve the status quo through changes in structure, orientation, and the "strategic concept" underlying the mix of active and reserve forces in the U.S. Army. Confining this study to the Army is not meant to disparage the other services, of course. But the contemporary issues involving the Army reserves are unique, given their unusually heavy and still growing role in conventional force planning. The issues facing the other services' reserve components, while also deserving attention, are less compelling.

Finally, a note about terminology. The terms *reserves* and *reserve forces* are used interchangeably in this study to mean all the reserve units and reservists under the purview of a military service, for example, both the Army Reserve and the Army National Guard. When the term is capitalized, as in Army Reserve, the reference is to that specific component alone.

CHAPTER TWO

THE ARMY RESERVES TODAY

THE ARMY reserve components are among the nation's most venerable institutions, rich with legacies dating from early colonial times.[1] The relatively simple militia of the seventeenth century, however, has gone through complex changes in institutional relationships, conditions of membership, and roles and missions. This evolution has produced a contemporary reserve that bears little resemblance to its antecedents.

Today's Army reserve establishment is, in fact, two organizations—the Army National Guard and the Army Reserve—with widely diverse memberships totaling more than one and a half million people. Though most reservists belong to units, many do not. Most of them train regularly and get paid, but some do neither. Most are part-time citizen-soldiers, but a large and growing number are full-time cadre. Although many reservists can be called to duty at the discretion of the president, some can be mobilized only through an act of Congress. And, under current wartime planning, while most Army reservists would be used only as reinforcements during a major conflict, a growing number would be needed earlier, some for even "minor" contingencies.

1. For accounts of the evolution of the National Guard and Reserve organizations, see John K. Mahon, *History of the Militia and the National Guard* (Macmillan, 1983); Martha Derthick, *The National Guard in Politics* (Harvard University Press, 1965); William H. Riker, *Soldiers of the States: The Role of the National Guard in American Democracy* (Washington, D.C.: Public Affairs Press, 1957; New York: Arno Press, 1979); and William F. Levantrosser, *Congress and the Citizen-Soldier: Legislative Policy-making for the Federal Armed Forces Reserve* (Ohio State University Press, 1967). For a concise summary, see Robert L. Goldich, "Historical Continuity in the US Military Reserve System," in Bennie J. Wilson III, ed., *The Guard and Reserve in the Total Force: The First Decade, 1973–1983* (Washington, D.C.: National Defense University Press, 1985), pp. 9–27.

Table 2-1. Strength of Army Reserve Components, by Category, March 1988
Strength in thousands

Category	Army National Guard	Army Reserve	Total
Ready Reserve	**459.0**	**601.0**	**1,060.1**
Selected Reserve	449.0	315.1	764.2
Part-time reservists	399.4	297.2	696.6
Full-time reservists	49.6	17.9	67.6
Active Guard/Reserve	25.0	12.4	37.4
Military technicians	24.6	5.5	30.1
Individual Ready Reserve	. . .	285.9	285.9
Inactive National Guard	10.0	. . .	10.0
Standby Reserve	a	**1.1**	**1.1**
Retired Reserve	b	**622.1**c	**622.1**
Total reserves	**459.0**	**1,224.2**	**1,683.2**

Source: Adapted from Assistant Secretary of Defense (Reserve Affairs), *Official Guard and Reserve Manpower Strengths and Statistics, March 1988* (Department of Defense, 1988), p. 2. Figures are rounded.

a. The Army National Guard does not maintain a Standby Reserve category.

b. Members of the National Guard who qualify for retirement are transferred to the Army Retired Reserve.

c. Includes roughly 350,000 retirees who served on active duty for at least twenty years.

Organization

U.S. Army reservists belong to one of the two components, the Army National Guard (459,013 members) or the Army Reserve (602,135, not including those on the retired rolls; figures in this section are as of March 1988 unless otherwise noted). Control of the Army Reserve is unambiguously vested in the federal government, while the Army National Guard, which is organized by state, is under the control of governors except when activated for federal purposes under the authorities given the president and Congress.[2] The two components also have somewhat different roles and missions: the National Guard is chiefly a combat force, whereas the Reserve is mainly a support force.

Besides being divided along federal and state lines, reservists are also identified with one of three readiness categories—Ready Reserve, Standby Reserve, and Retired Reserve—distinguishable by their preparedness and their susceptibility to call-up. (Table 2-1 compares their strength).

The *Ready Reserve* has by far the largest share of total Army reserve

2. The question of control has always been controversial. It became especially prominent during school desegregation in the 1960s and surfaced again in the mid-1980s when several governors refused to permit members of their National Guard units to participate in training exercises in Central America. This event is discussed more fully in chapter 5.

manpower (nearly 63 percent) and the bulk of the reserve forces' capabilities. The Ready Reserve, in turn, is made up of the Selected Reserve, Individual Ready Reserve (IRR), and Inactive National Guard (ING). The Selected Reserve, with just over 45 percent of all Army reservists, consists mainly of soldiers in organized units of the Army National Guard or Army Reserve who train periodically and who are paid.[3] Typically, Army Guard and Reserve units drill one weekend a month and train two weeks during the summer.[4]

Although more than 90 percent of Selected Reserve soldiers are part-timers, some serve on a full-time basis. Included are Active Guard/Reserve (AGR) personnel, who are reservists on active duty providing full-time support to their reserve units, and military technicians (MTs), who maintain military reservist and civil service status simultaneously. The latter generally serve the reserve unit in their civil service capacity except during drills and annual training and, of course, when mobilized.

Members of the IRR are soldiers who have earlier served and been trained in either the active or reserve Army but who no longer belong to a unit, and generally neither train nor get paid. These soldiers are either fulfilling their remaining enlistment obligation or contractual commitment, or have voluntarily extended their affiliation with the IRR. Members of the ING, the Guard's counterpart to the IRR, do not train regularly but are attached to specific National Guard units with which they are required to muster once a year. Last year the Army's IRR consisted of about

3. The Selected Reserve also includes a small number (about 13,000) of trained individuals in the Individual Mobilization Augmentee (IMA) program, under which the reservist is not a member of a unit but is assigned to a billet in the active Army, the Selective Service System, or the Federal Emergency Management Agency. IMAs typically perform two weeks of annual training with the unit, and some may attend training drills. For the manpower figure, see Assistant Secretary of Defense (Reserve Affairs), *Official Guard and Reserve Manpower Strengths and Statistics, March 1988* (Department of Defense, 1988), p. 2. For a description of the IMA program, see *Reserve Component Programs, Fiscal Year 1987: Annual Report of the Reserve Forces Policy Board*, pp. 46–47.

4. Members of Army reserve units are required to participate each year in a minimum of forty-eight drill periods. A drill period (or unit training assembly—UTA) is nominally four hours long, and the reserve unit will usually carry out four drills during a two-day weekend each month. One day's pay and one retirement point are authorized for each drill period. Annual training must be a continuous period, usually lasting fourteen days (exclusive of travel time) for the Army Reserve and fifteen days (including travel time) for the Army National Guard. Additional information on the composition and duties of the reserve components can be found in *Reserve Forces Almanac, 1987,* 13th ed. (Washington, D.C.: Uniformed Services Almanac, 1987).

286,00 men and women, while the ING had about 10,000 members (table 2-1).

Of the three Ready Reserve categories, the Selected Reserve is the most easily mobilized for nondomestic purposes. The president can call up, by executive order alone, as many as 200,000 of its members for 90 days or, under certain conditions, for 180 days. A larger mobilization of selected reservists, or one involving the Individual Ready Reserve, requires a presidential proclamation of a national emergency. Under this authority, up to a million members of the entire Ready Reserve (Selected Reserve or IRR/ING) can be called, but for not more than twenty-four consecutive months. Finally, a full mobilization of the Ready Reserve requires the passage of a public law or joint resolution by Congress declaring war or a national emergency. (See appendix A for a summary of mobilization authority.)

The *Standby Reserve* consists of people who do not train or get paid, and its members can be called to active duty only in time of war or national emergency declared by Congress (see appendix A). Once a major repository of men fulfilling required military obligations, this pool has dwindled to a trivial fraction of the reserves as the Army has emphasized the accession and retention of personnel in the Ready Reserves. In 1988 only 1,091 Standby Reserve members were on the Army's rolls (table 2-1), mainly key civilian employees and reservists with temporary hardships or disabilities.

The *Retired Reserve* includes all Army reserve officers who receive retirement pay; all reserve officers and enlisted reservists who are otherwise eligible for retirement pay but have not reached the age of 60, have not elected discharge, and are not voluntary members of the Ready or Standby Reserve; and enlisted personnel who have completed twenty or more years but less than thirty years of active duty.[5] Last year about 622,000 soldiers were on the retired rolls (table 2-1), of which 350,000 had completed at least twenty years of active duty. Under certain conditions, retirees can be recalled to active duty, a possibility that has

5. Office of the Assistant Secretary of Defense (Reserve Affairs), "Reserve Category Definitions," November 19, 1985, p. 8. Members of the reserves may retire after twenty years of "creditable" service, the last eight of which must be in a reserve component. Reserve retired pay is not payable, however, until the member reaches 60 years of age. The amount of retired pay is based on grade and on years of service determined by a point system. A point is awarded for each drill attended or for a day of service, and fifteen points are awarded for a year's membership. A "creditable" year is one in which the member earns at least fifty points.

received more attention in recent years as the IRR has shrunk.[6] For estimating mobilization potential, the Department of Defense classifies retirees according to age, years retired, and disability status. The most vulnerable to recall would be nondisabled reservists under 60 who have been retired for five years or less.

Force Structure

Counting reservists, whatever their status, provides only the total number of bodies available for mobilization. The more important question relates to output: what capabilities do these manpower resources represent?

The force structure of the Army reserves is a convenient framework for understanding their numerous missions and functions. The Army reserve components have more than 7,700 units, ranging from National Guard divisions with about 16,000 members to reserve detachments with fewer than a half-dozen. Their responsibilities span the full spectrum of military combat and support activities (table 2-2). Generally speaking, the Army National Guard is charged with combat missions, while the Army Reserve supports the combat forces.

In 1988 National Guard forces included ten combat divisions, eighteen maneuver units, three medical brigades, four armored cavalry regiments, two special forces groups, four antitank battalions, five scout battalions, and one mountain infantry battalion.[7] In addition, five brigades and seven battalions of the National Guard now "round out" active Army divisions, that is, raise understructured active divisions to full wartime configuration. These National Guard round-out units, which have close planning and training relations with their parent units in the active Army, are expected to deploy with them and, in theory at least, share their priority ranking when resources are being allocated. Currently, of the eighteen active Army divisions, four contain both a National Guard brigade and a battalion, one is rounded out by a National Guard brigade, and three others are rounded out by National Guard battalions. The Army National Guard is thus represented in eighteen of a total of twenty-eight Army combat divisions.

6. For these conditions, see 10 U.S.C. 688.
7. *Reserve Component Programs, Fiscal Year 1987: Annual Report of the Reserve Forces Policy Board*, p. 5.

Table 2-2. Distribution of Selected Military Units, by Army Component, September 30, 1987
Percent of total Army

Type of unit	Active Army	Army National Guard	Army Reserve
Combat			
Combat divisions	64	36	0
Separate brigades	21	66	13
Armored cavalry regiments	43	57	0
Mechanized infantry battalions	51	47	2
Armored battalions	55	43	2
Infantry battalions	18	74	8
Light antitank infantry battalions	0	100	0
Infantry scout groups	0	100	0
Support			
Training divisions and brigades	0	0	100
Railroad units	0	0	100
Civil affairs units	3	0	97
Maintenance companies	11	46	43
Supply and service units	10	31	59
Combat engineer units	33	43	24
Truck companies	33	37	30
Conventional ammunition companies	32	17	51

Source: Adapted from *Reserve Component Programs, Fiscal Year 1987: Annual Report of the Reserve Forces Policy Board*, p. 6.

The Army Reserve, on the other hand, provides only three separate brigades (including one round-out) and thirteen maneuver battalions (including two round-out).[8] For the most part it consists of myriad and sundry small combat-support and combat-service-support units. The contrast between the missions of the active Army and its Guard and Reserve components is sharp, as shown by the combat-support mix in each (percentage of authorized manpower by function):[9]

Function	Active Army	Army National Guard	Army Reserve
Combat	52	71	19
Support	48	29	81

8. Comptroller of the Army, *The Army Budget, Fiscal Year 1988–89* (Department of the Army, February 1987), p. 68.

9. "Statement of General John A. Wickham, Jr., Chief of Staff, U.S. Army," in *Department of Defense Authorization for Appropriations for Fiscal Year 1987,* Hearings before the Senate Committee on Armed Services, 99 Cong. 2 sess. (Government Printing Office, 1986), pt. 3, p. 895.

Figure 2-1. Total Army Structure, Fiscal Year 1987

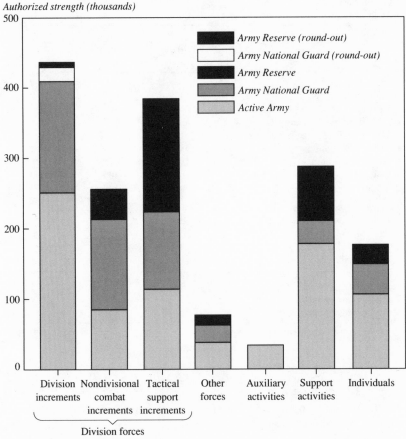

Authorized strength (thousands)

Legend:
- Army Reserve (round-out)
- Army National Guard (round-out)
- Army Reserve
- Army National Guard
- Active Army

Categories: Division increments · Nondivisional combat increments · Tactical support increments · Other forces · Auxiliary activities · Support activities · Individuals

Division forces (Division increments, Nondivisional combat increments, Tactical support increments)

Source: See table 2-3.

Another perspective on the roles of the reserve components can be gained by seeing how they fit into the Total Army structure. Figure 2-1 and table 2-3 display total Army manpower grouped by force planning and programming categories. The figure clearly shows that the bulk of total Army manpower is in the *division forces*. Because actual combat divisions and their support units vary somewhat with mission, environment, and tempo of operations, the Army uses a division force equivalent (DFE) standard, a notional portrayal of a typical combat division and the nondivisional combat, administrative, and logistical support units deployed into a combat theater to sustain combat operations. The DFE is made up of three elements:

1. *Division increments,* the combat maneuver battalions and a division

Table 2-3. Distribution of Army Manpower, by Component and Defense Planning and Programming Categories, Fiscal Year 1987[a]
Authorized strength in thousands[b]

Category	Active Army	Army National Guard	Army Reserve	Total Army
Division forces	**438.0**	**409.9**	**204.0**	**1,051.9**
Division increments	244.2	175.0	6.8	426.0
Active Army (18)	244.2	17.7[c]	} 6.8[d]	} 426.0
National Guard (10)	. . .	157.3		
Nondivisional combat increments	81.5	127.2	41.8	250.5
Tactical support increments	112.3	107.7	155.4	375.4
Other forces[e]	**38.5**	**20.9**	**14.4**	**73.8**
Auxiliary activities[f]	**29.5**	**0.0**	**0.7**	**30.2**
Support activities[g]	**172.4**	**31.5**	**75.8**	**279.7**
Individuals[h]	**102.3**	**39.8**	**27.4**	**169.5**
Totals	**780.7**	**502.1**	**322.3**	**1,605.1**

Source: Based on data derived from Program Objective Memorandum 88-92 as cited in the factsheet "Total Army Structure—FY 1987," obtained from the Department of the Army, March 1987. Figures are rounded.

a. Only the Selected Reserve is included in the figures for the two reserve components.

b. "Authorized" is distinct from "operating" or "actual" strength, shown in table 2-1. The difference is especially apparent in the Army National Guard.

c. Reservists assigned to units that round out active Army divisions.

d. Army Reserve units round out both active and National Guard divisions. Their contribution to the latter consists mainly of military intelligence units.

e. Consists of theater, mobility, and strategic forces.

f. Army support of defense-wide intelligence, centrally managed communications, research and development, and geophysical activities.

g. Base-operating support functions for Army installations; centralized medical, personnel, training, and logistics; and management headquarters.

h. Trainees, students, and personnel traveling between assignments.

base made up of combat-support units (artillery, air defense) as well as combat-service-support units (supply and transportation, medical, maintenance).

2. *Nondivisional combat increments,* separate combat brigades and nondivisional artillery, aviation, and combat engineer units.

3. *Tactical support increments,* additional combat-support and combat-service-support units needed to sustain the division and the nondivisional combat increments in the theater of operations (military police, signal, medical, construction, logistics units).

For planning purposes, a DFE by definition has 48,000 soldiers; 16,000 in the division increment, 12,000 in the nondivisional combat increment, and 20,000 in the tactical support increment.[10]

The divisional forces are by far the largest consumer of Army trained

10. Department of the Army, *Army Reference Data Handbook* (Carlisle Barracks, Penn.: U.S. Army War College, 1984), p. 30.

manpower, accounting for close to three-fourths of the total; the bulk of the rest operate Army installations worldwide, sustain deployed forces with equipment, supplies, and troop replacements, and provide resources for mobilization and expansion of the force.

The Army's reserve components contribute heavily to division force manpower, accounting for close to 60 percent of the total. The ten divisions of the Army National Guard, along with its separate round-out units, represent over 40 percent of the Army's total manpower for combat division forces, and roughly half of the total manpower for nondivisional combat forces. By contrast, Army Reserve participation in division increments is minimal, accounting for under 2 percent of total combat division manpower. The Army Reserve too provides some nondivisional combat forces, but its major contribution is to the tactical support increment, supplying more than 40 percent of Army troops assigned to those units (see table 2-3).

Taking all combat units into consideration, one can see that the Army National Guard and Reserve, while owning only 10 division flags, constitute 17⅔ division-equivalents in the active Army. In these terms, then, the reserves account for roughly half of the Army's divisional unit count.[11]

As mentioned earlier, the Army leans heavily on its reserve components for combat support and combat service support. The reserves account for 89 percent of maintenance companies, 90 percent of supply and service units, 67 percent of combat engineer units, 67 percent of truck companies, and 68 percent of conventional ammunition companies (table 2-2). For some missions, such as those performed by railroad units, the capabilities lie exclusively with the reserves, though these are generally lower-priority activities.

Deployment Requirements

The reserve components now bear not only a large responsibility for the Army's warfighting mission but an early one as well. Before the Total

11. A simple static count of divisions or division-equivalents, it should be noted, is an inadequate and often misleading measure of military capability. Few would contend, for example, that the combat performance of a National Guard division would be on a par with its active counterparts. Relative capabilities of active and reserve units, which depend on differences in manning, equipment, and training, can be assessed through firepower and effectiveness measures. One means for doing this is discussed in chapter 7 and appendix C.

Force policy, the reserves were viewed as late-deploying reinforcements for a protracted conflict. Today, reserve units are scheduled to deploy within the first few days or weeks of mobilization.

For the most demanding contingency—a war in Central Europe—Pentagon plans assume that within ten days the $4\frac{2}{3}$ American divisions already in place in Europe would be augmented by 6 divisions from the United States, whose equipment sets are already pre-positioned in Europe.[12] After the first ten days, reinforcements would be committed on a timetable dictated by the ability to move people and equipment. Presumably, 2 more fully equipped divisions could be airlifted to Europe within thirty days, after which forces would begin arriving via sealift. Force planners have assumed that, between ten and ninety days after mobilization, a total of 13 division-equivalents would have reached the war zone.[13]

How many of these forces would be reservists? The active-reserve mix cannot be predicted with any certainty, but according to the latest publicly available version of the Army's deployment sequence (fiscal 1983), two of the six divisions expected to reach Europe within ten days would arrive without their National Guard round-out brigades, which would not join up until M + 29 days (see appendix B).[14] Under this plan the first reserve combat units to arrive in the theater would be two infantry brigades to augment the already deployed 1st Infantry and 4th Infantry divisions.[15] The first National Guard divisions would not reach Europe for fifty-seven days, with a total of seven arriving within seventy-nine days.

This sequence, however, is somewhat at odds with more recent statements by reserve officials, who contend that four of the ten National

12. *Department of Defense Annual Report to the Congress, Fiscal Year 1986*, p. 224. Because of shortages in airlift and sealift assets, the ability of the United States to field ten Army divisions in Europe in ten days has been in question, as has the ability to move enough ammunition and supplies through the crowded metropolitan areas to support them. According to press accounts, the commander-in-chief of the U.S. Army in Europe, General Glenn K. Otis, has estimated that it would take at least thirty days "to deploy the needed U.S. forces to Europe." David Fulghum, "Airlift, Sealift Capability Severely Lacking: Cassidy," *Navy Times*, April 25, 1988, p. 29.

13. William P. Mako, *U.S. Ground Forces and the Defense of Central Europe* (Brookings, 1983), pp. 52–54.

14. This schedule has since been altered. The 24th Infantry Division, for example, is now earmarked for the U.S. Central Command (CENTCOM), as discussed later.

15. Unlike round-out units, augmentation units add capabilities to *fully* constituted combat divisions. Under this plan the 32d Infantry Brigade, for example, would be a fourth brigade assigned to the 1st Infantry Division.

Guard divisions and eight of their fourteen separate brigades would be deployed by M + 60 and five additional divisions by M + 90.[16] Under this schedule, roughly half of the combat forces deployed by M + 90 would be National Guard troops.

The chief Army Reserve contribution in the early days of a European conflict would be combat-support and combat-service-support units needed to fill existing gaps in the M-day force. Army divisions deployed in Europe have only enough organic combat service support to fight for about seven days, so nondivisional support units would have to be mobilized and deployed within a few days of the outbreak of hostilities.[17] Planners estimate the reserves would have to provide about half the tactical logistics support needed by the M-day force and more than 75 percent of the support required by the six-division augmentation force.[18] All told, 30 percent of all Army Reserve units would have to be mobilized within thirty days, 50 to 60 percent within sixty days, and virtually all within ninety days.[19]

Looking at the overall picture, the Congressional Budget Office estimates that among Army forces committed during the first month of a war in Europe, the reserves would make up about 10 percent of the combat units, 60 percent of the combat-support units, and 58 percent of the combat-service-support units. Altogether the 300,000 reservists would constitute 42 percent of all Army troops deployed in the first month.[20] These early demands on U.S. reserve units are expected to diminish as recently negotiated Wartime Host-Nation Support agreements are carried out. Under the current agreement with the West German government, for example, about 49,000 German reservists will eventually be available to provide such services as transportation,

16. "Statement by Lieutenant General Herbert R. Temple, Jr., Chief, National Guard Bureau, before the Subcommittee on Manpower and Personnel of the Senate Committee on Armed Services," 100 Cong. 1 sess., March 3, 1987, p. 5.

17. See Charles D. Odorizzi and Benjamin F. Schemmer, "An Exclusive *AFJ* Interview with General Glenn K. Otis," *Armed Forces Journal International,* January 1987, p. 48.

18. Norman E. Betaque, Jr., "Reservations about the Reserves," *Military Logistics Forum,* vol. 1 (March 1985), p. 38.

19. Warren W. Lenhart, *The Mix of United States Active and Reserve Forces* (Washington, D.C.: Congressional Research Service, August 1983), p. 29.

20. Congressional Budget Office, *Improving the Army Reserves* (November 1985), p. 23.

resupply, casualty evacuation, decontamination, and installation security to the U.S. Army in Europe.[21]

A war in Europe would also quickly generate a need for members of the Individual Ready Reserve to fill out active U.S. Army units, few of which are fully manned in peacetime. Only 7 percent of active combat battalions are authorized 100 percent of their troops, about three-quarters of them are at 90 percent, and about 18 percent are at or below the 80 percent manning level. On the support side, more than a third of the combat-service-support companies in the active Army are at or below the 80 percent level.[22] By one estimate the Army would need more than 25,000 soldiers just to fill vacancies in its deployed M-day force, which, despite its high priority, has few fully manned units.[23] IRR members would also be needed to fill out mobilized reserve units, most of which are authorized less manpower and equipment than similar active units. As of 1983, for example, all of the National Guard's divisions, and three of its four round-out brigades, had only 80 percent of their authorized manpower for wartime. In 1984 about half of the Army Reserve's combat-service-support companies were at this level or below.[24]

During large-scale conflict, IRR soldiers would also be among the first troops called on to replace combat casualties, at least until the Army was able to enlist or conscript new recruits, train them, and deploy them. This process, even with draft registration in place, is expected to take

21. "Wartime Host Nation Support (WHNS) in Germany," factsheet obtained from the Department of the Army, October 1986. Many observers have expressed concern about American dependence on other nations to support U.S. forces. See, for example, James Kitfield, "The Host-Nation Support Gamble," *Military Logistics Forum,* vol. 4 (October 1987), pp. 30–36. And it remains to be seen whether West Germans will be able to satisfy these commitments over the longer term, when their declining youth population is expected to create manpower shortages. For a discussion of this issue, see François L. Heisbourg, "Conventional Defense: Europe's Constraints and Opportunities," in Andrew J. Pierre, ed., *The Conventional Defense of Europe: New Technologies and New Strategies* (New York: Council on Foreign Relations, 1986), pp. 73–77.

22. Department of Defense, "Reserve and National Guard Capabilities," Report to the Senate Committee on Armed Services, March 19, 1984, p. 16.

23. *Department of Defense Appropriations for 1985,* Hearings before a Subcommittee of the House Committee on Appropriations, 98 Cong. 2 sess. (GPO, 1984), pt. 1, pp. 683–84, 689. In fact, "of 16 active divisions, . . . it is expected that only two will be fully combat ready" (p. 683).

24. Ibid., p. 697; and Department of Defense, "Reserve and National Guard Capabilities," p. 16.

more than a hundred days. Estimates of how many casualty replacements will be needed in the first ninety days have risen steadily. For example, in fiscal 1980 the Army estimated that 189,000 casualties would be incurred if war broke out that year, with projections growing to nearly 400,000 casualties if war broke out in fiscal 1987.[25] Predicting when casualties will occur is hard because so much depends on the kind of operations, but clearly the heaviest casualties are expected in the early days of a European war. If members of the IRR are to fill those needs, many would have to be available within days of the outbreak of hostilities.

Plans for the early involvement of the reserves are not limited to the NATO contingency. The Army Reserve, in fact, would figure prominently in the deployment of forces of the U.S. Central Command (CENTCOM), which started life in 1980 as the "Rapid Deployment Joint Task Force" (RDJTF). From a modest initial contribution of 83 transportation, fuel, and civil affairs support units, the Reserve's role had increased by 1983 to 189 units, including military police, public affairs, and signal corps units, all ticketed for the rapid deployment mission.[26] The current composition of CENTCOM forces is classified, but the reserve contribution has probably grown substantially since then. For example, the 48th Infantry Brigade (Georgia National Guard) rounds out the 24th Infantry Division, which is now earmarked for CENTCOM.

The sequence in which units under CENTCOM control might actually be deployed would depend on the specific contingency, but as of 1983 (the latest date for which unclassified data are available), the Army's potential contribution amounted to roughly 130,000 troops in the following major units: Headquarters, U.S. Army Central Command (Third U.S. Army), 18th Airborne Corps Headquarters, 82d Airborne Division,

25. Reserve Forces Policy Board, *Fiscal Year 1981 Readiness Assessment of the Reserve Components* (Department of Defense, Office of the Secretary of Defense, 1981), p. 33.

26. See Dick Crossland, "RDJTF: Can It Get There without the USAR?" *Army Reserve Magazine*, vol. 28 (Spring 1982), p. 9; and Richard B. Crossland and James T. Currie, *Twice the Citizen: A History of the United States Army Reserve, 1908–1983* (Washington, D.C.: Office of the Chief, Army Reserve, 1984), p. 269. That the reserves have any role, much less a prominent one, in CENTCOM force planning has not been widely noticed. In fact, one survey taken in 1982 among students at the Industrial College of the Armed Forces and the National War College revealed that 77 percent of the former and 76 percent of the latter did not know that reserve units were part of CENTCOM. The military students, it should be noted, were senior lieutenant colonels and junior colonels. See James W. Browning II and others, "The US Reserve System: Attitudes, Perceptions, and Realities," in Wilson, ed., *Guard and Reserve in the Total Force*, pp. 80–81.

Table 2-4. U.S. Army Budget Allocations to Active and Reserve Forces, Fiscal Years 1987–89
Total obligational authority in billions of current dollars

Component	1987	1988	1989
Active Army	67.5	70.9	73.7
Army National Guard	5.0	5.3	5.5
Army Reserve	3.0	3.3	3.4
Total Army	75.5	79.4	82.6
	Reserve components' budget as a percent of total Army budget		
Addendum	10.6	10.7	10.8

Source: Comptroller of the Army, *The Army Budget, Fiscal Year 1988–89* (Department of the Army, February 1987), p. 45. Figures are rounded.

101st Airborne Division (air assault), 24th Infantry Division (mechanized), 6th Cavalry Brigade (air combat), and 1st Corps Support Command.[27] We cannot give a firm figure for how many reserve units or troops would be involved, but one clue to how heavily CENTCOM would depend on the reserves was given in 1981 by Lieutenant General Robert C. Kingston, the RDJTF commander at the time, who estimated that "a substantial deployment of the RDJTF would require the President to exercise all or part of his authority to call 100,000 Reservists and Guardsmen to active duty."[28]

Costs

The formidable responsibilities vested in the Army's reserve components seem all the more impressive when one considers the relatively small share of the Army's budget allocated to the reserves. Official data show that the Army is currently spending roughly 11 percent of its budget on its reserve components, with close to 7 percent going to the National Guard and just over 4 percent to the Army Reserve (table 2-4).

In fact, however, the full cost of the Army reserve is difficult to pin down. The most significant of the nonvisible budget items is the cost of equipment, both new and used, that is issued to the reserves. In the case of new equipment, such as the M1 tanks being delivered to some reserve

27. U.S. Central Command, *U.S. Central Command: Making a Major Contribution toward Peace, Stability and Security in a Vital Region* (January 1983), p. 5.
28. Cited in Crossland, "RDJTF," p. 9.

units, the costs appear in Army procurement accounts.[29] And the value of equipment inherited from the active forces is not charged to the reserves. Although the cost of hand-me-downs is usually viewed as sunk, it does, however, represent an opportunity cost. If the active forces continued to use the equipment, their modernization could be postponed, though perhaps at some loss in military capability. Alternatively, the equipment could conceivably be sold to foreign nations or provided to them under military assistance programs. It is difficult to impute these costs with precision, but the Army has estimated that the equipment distributed to the Army National Guard in fiscal 1986 was worth $1.6 billion, while the Army Reserve received equipment valued at just over $200 million in the same year.[30]

Also hidden are the costs associated with the activities of the active forces that support reserve units. These would include, for example, the base operating costs for an active Army installation providing services to both active and reserve units. These costs, it should be noted, would be offset to some extent by costs absorbed by reserve forces in support of active units (for example, reservists maintaining active Army equipment). At any rate, the advertised Army reserve budget is understated, with the extent depending mainly on the budgetary cost of new equipment and the opportunity cost of inherited equipment.

Summary

By virtually any measure, the Army reserves of the late 1980s bear unprecedented levels of responsibility for the defense of the United

29. Separate procurement accounts do not exist for the Army National Guard or Army Reserve. But in fiscal 1982 Congress set up a special Department of Defense appropriation account entitled "National Guard and Reserve Equipment Appropriations" (also known as the Dedicated Procurement Program) to cover all reserve components. Each year since, Congress has dedicated appropriations, additional to those requested by the administration, for reserve procurement. In fiscal 1986, for example, $532 million and $365 million were earmarked for the Army National Guard and Army Reserve, respectively. For fiscal 1987, the figures dropped to $146 million and $90 million. See *Reserve Component Programs, Fiscal Year 1987: Annual Report of the Reserve Forces Policy Board*, pp. 79–80.

30. "Statement by Brigadier General Richard D. Dean, Acting Director, Army National Guard, before the Subcommittee on Manpower and Personnel of the Senate Committee on Armed Services," 100 Cong. 1 sess., March 3, 1987, p. 16; and Major General William F. Ward, chief, Army Reserve, *The Posture of the Army Reserve— FY88* (U.S. Army Reserve), p. 49. These estimates are based upon year-to-year changes in the total asset value of reserve equipment.

States. They are at their peak peacetime strength; they are assigned missions vital to both the warfighting capability and sustainability of the U.S. Army; and many of their units are expected to deploy on as tight a timetable as active units. Indeed, as matters stand, the military operations that the Army could conduct without involving its reserve components appear to be extremely limited.

CHAPTER THREE

FACTORS SHAPING THE ARMY RESERVES

AMERICAN MILITARY planners have not always given Army reservists responsibilities as prominent as those described in the previous chapter. Indeed, for twenty-five years after the Second World War, the Army's reserve components were viewed as second-stringers, "to be held in the background, usually in a subordinate role and assigned secondary missions, until mobilized in the later and more desperate stages of the national military crisis."[1] As such, reserve units did not fare well in the competition for resources and were typically underequipped and poorly trained, shortcomings that became obvious in the partial mobilizations ordered for the Korean War in 1950 and the Berlin crisis in 1961, and after the *Pueblo* and Tet incidents in 1968.[2]

The Vietnam era, in fact, was a particularly dismal period for the Army's reserve forces. With minor exceptions, its units were not called upon to take part in the longest war in the nation's history. The reserves thus became a haven for draft-averse "volunteers" seeking to avoid service in Vietnam.[3] Reserve units were stripped of essential equipment needed for the active forces, and reserve training came to a virtual standstill. By the end of the 1960s, according to the official historical

1. Edward J. Philbin and James L. Gould, "The Guard and Reserve: In Pursuit of Full Integration," in Bennie J. Wilson III, ed., *The Guard and Reserve in the Total Force: The First Decade, 1973–1983* (Washington, D.C.: National Defense University Press, 1985), pp. 44–45.
2. These mobilizations are discussed in chapter 4.
3. An estimated 70 percent of reserve enlistments were prompted by the threat of the draft. Gus C. Lee and Geoffrey Y. Parker, *Ending the Draft: The Story of the All Volunteer Force*, FR-PO-77-1 (Alexandria, Va.: Human Resources Research Organization, April 1977), p. 41.

account, the Army Reserve was in "disrepair and disarray," and its "ability to go to war was near zero."[4]

By the turn of the decade, however, as the nation began to disengage from its military involvement in Southeast Asia and to fashion its post-Vietnam military establishment, the reserve forces, tarnished image and all, figured prominently. The Nixon administration's launching of the Total Force concept in 1970 ushered in a reserve renaissance of sorts, leading to a Total Army force structure distinctly different from its recent predecessors and especially conspicuous for its heavy and early reliance on reserves.

It would be comforting to assume that the current mix of active and reserve Army forces and missions was the product of a sound planning process within which decisions were based on cost and effectiveness considerations. In fact, however, the current Army structure has evolved in bits and pieces and apparently without any grand strategic design. That much was admitted by the Department of Defense in its response to a request in 1983 by the Senate Armed Services Committee for a "justification of the current mix of active and Reserve units and missions in the force structure."[5] The Pentagon replied that "the Department's major analytical effort to date on the active/reserve force mix has focused on the basis for decisions on the margin. . . . A comprehensive, top down analysis of force mix is not available now."[6] Despite this limited perspective, the guidance issued to the military services in 1983 by the secretary of defense stipulated that "military units added to the programmed force will be placed in the RCs (Reserve Components) unless overseas stationing, peacetime operations or the responsiveness needed in war dictate otherwise."[7]

It may be extreme to conclude, as has a former Pentagon insider, that the nation is staking its "external security on a reserve component structure that is better explained by domestic politics than by military

4. Richard B. Crossland and James T. Currie, *Twice the Citizen: A History of the United States Army Reserve, 1908–1983* (Washington, D.C.: Office of the Chief, Army Reserve, 1984), p. 211.

5. *Omnibus Defense Authorization Act, 1984,* S. Rept. 98-174, 98 Cong. 1 sess. (Government Printing Office, 1983), p. 190.

6. Department of Defense, "Reserve and National Guard Capabilities," Report to the Senate Committee on Armed Services, March 19, 1984, p. 3.

7. Quoted in Edward D. Simms, Jr., and others, *Total Force Composition: Improving the Force-Mix Management Process* (Washington, D.C.: Logistics Management Institute, February 1984), p. 2–3.

strategy,"[8] but it is clear that the mix of active and reserve is shaped by many factors not directly related to military necessity. An understanding of these factors is essential to an appreciation of the options for, and constraints upon, future change.

The End of Conscription and Major Force Reductions

The one event most responsible for breathing life back into the reserves in the early 1970s was the end of the draft. Conceived during Richard Nixon's 1968 presidential campaign, the move to abolish the draft was formalized with the creation in 1969 of the President's Commission on an All-Volunteer Armed Force (popularly called the Gates Commission after its chairman, former Secretary of Defense Thomas S. Gates), with a charter to develop a plan for eliminating the draft and moving toward an all-volunteer force. In its report of February 1970, the commission concluded: "We unanimously believe that the nation's interest will be better served by an all-volunteer force. . . . We have satisfied ourselves that a volunteer force will not jeopardize national security, and we believe it will have a beneficial effect on the military as well as the rest of our society."[9] The commission suggested an end to induction authority by June 30, 1971, but the administration sought, and Congress approved, a two-year extension, to June 30, 1973.

With the end of conscription, the nation abandoned a system characterized by persistent underpayment of personnel for one based on competitive market forces. The element of the "free good" in military manpower had been eliminated. In effect the new system put a ceiling on the size of the armed forces, lest manpower costs exact a prohibitive toll on the defense budget. Although the Gates Commission refrained from proposing an exact size for the all-volunteer force, it explored a range from 2 million to 3 million men and recommended pay increases "designed to provide . . . the quantity and quality of volunteers required

8. James L. Lacy, "Whither the All-Volunteer Force?" *Yale Law and Policy Review*, vol. 5 (Fall–Winter 1986), p. 67.
9. *The Report of the President's Commission on an All-Volunteer Armed Force* (GPO, 1970), p. iii.

for an overall force level of approximately 2.5 million men," of which roughly one million would be in the Army.[10]

Along with ending conscription, the incoming Nixon administration changed the force-planning ground rules by adopting a "one-and-a-half-war" strategy in place of the "two-and-a-half-war" strategy that had presumably shaped the pre-Vietnam force structure.[11] As explained by President Nixon, the United States would henceforth "maintain in peacetime general purpose forces adequate for simultaneously meeting a major Communist attack in *either* Europe or Asia, assisting allies against non-Chinese threats in Asia, and contending with a [minor] contingency elsewhere." What had prompted the change? The president noted that "prospects for a coordinated two-front attack on our allies by Russia and China" had diminished as a result of the risks of escalation to nuclear war, on the one hand, and the deteriorated state of Sino-Soviet relations, on the other.[12] Budgetary pressures played a role, too. Perhaps most important, the fact that a smaller Army would require fewer recruits and thus could ease the transition to a volunteer force was not lost on administration officials.[13]

Whatever the reasons, by 1972 the Army had been pared to thirteen active divisions and roughly 800,000 troops—the smallest it had been since 1950. The substantial decline in Army strength enabled the administration to issue the last draft calls in December 1972, six months ahead

10. Ibid., pp. 5, 57, 37. This estimate was consistent with the strength considered necessary to field the sixteen active divisions contemplated for the post-Vietnam Army. The commission used "men" to include both men and women. At that time, the role of women in the armed forces was still quite restricted, and the commission's report assumed that women would continue to make up about 1.2 percent of the post-Vietnam force. As matters turned out, had the services not expanded the role of women, it is doubtful that the volunteer system would have survived the 1970s. For further discussion of this point, see Martin Binkin and Mark J. Eitelberg, "Women and Minorities in the All-Volunteer Force," in William Bowman, Roger Little, and G. Thomas Sicilia, eds., *The All-Volunteer Force after a Decade: Retrospect and Prospect* (Pergamon-Brassey's, 1986), pp. 82–83.

11. There was a widespread view that in fact the United States had never fielded enough forces for a "two-and-a-half war" strategy. For a complete discussion of military force planning during that era, see William W. Kaufmann, *Planning Conventional Forces, 1950–80* (Brookings, 1982), especially pp. 4–17.

12. Richard Nixon, *U.S. Foreign Policy for the 1970s: A New Strategy for Peace*, Report to the Congress, February 1970 (GPO, 1970), p. 129. Emphasis added.

13. *Department of Defense Annual Report to the Congress, Fiscal Years 1976 and 197T*, p. III-14.

of schedule. In January of 1973, the system of conscription, a national fixture almost continuously since 1940, was officially put to rest by Secretary of Defense Melvin R. Laird: "The armed forces henceforth will depend exclusively on volunteer soldiers, sailors, airmen and marines. The use of the draft has ended."[14]

Total Force Planning

The end of the draft and the large force reductions had far-reaching implications for the Army's reserve components. To offset scaled-down active forces, the Nixon administration unveiled its Total Force concept. Secretary Laird explained the principle: "Emphasis will be given to concurrent consideration of the total forces, active and reserve, to determine the most advantageous mix to support national strategy and meet the threat. A total force concept will be applied in all aspects of planning, programming, manning, equipping and employing Guard and Reserve Forces."[15]

Widely perceived as the contemporary reserve forces' Magna Charta, the Laird memo clarified their expanded role: "Guard and Reservist units and individuals of the Selected Reserves will be prepared to be the initial and primary source for augmentation of the active forces in any future emergency requiring a rapid and substantial expansion of the active forces."

Finally, in recognition of problems that had plagued the reserves in the past, Laird spelled out what he expected of them, and what was to be done for them, in the future. The military services, he said, would:

> Increase the readiness, reliability and timely responsiveness of the combat and combat support units of the Guard and Reserve and individuals of the Reserve.
>
> Support and maintain minimum average trained strengths of the Selected Reserve as mandated by Congress.
>
> Provide and maintain combat standard equipment for Guard and Reserve units in the necessary quantities; and provide the necessary controls to

14. Quoted in David E. Rosenbaum, "Nation Ends Draft, Turns to Volunteers," *New York Times,* January 28, 1973, p. 1.

15. This and the following two quotations are from Memorandum from Secretary of Defense Melvin R. Laird to the Secretaries of the Military Departments, reprinted in *Congressional Record,* September 9, 1970, p. 30968.

identify resources committed for Guard and Reserve logistic support through the planning, programming, budgeting, procurement and distribution cycle.

The Army, meanwhile, was already considering plans to reorganize its command structure, prompted in part by concerns that the management of the reserve components was suffering at the hands of the "octopus-like" span of control of the Continental Army Command (CONARC). By 1972 the Army had decided to divide CONARC into the Forces Command and the Training and Doctrine Command; the main impact on the reserves was to be a complete overhaul in the way the active Army would advise, evaluate, and assist the Army reserves. Under the reorganization, which took effect on July 1, 1973, three Continental United States (CONUS) Army headquarters under the general direction of the Forces Command would provide readiness support through nine Army Readiness Regions. The regional elements consisted of active Army teams of branch and functional experts to provide on-the-spot readiness assistance.[16]

Though the Army was probably now better prepared organizationally to comply with the intent of the Total Force proclamation, it seemed reluctant to devote a larger share of its shrinking resources to its reserve components. The Army's allocation of resources seemed consistent with the "short war" scenario that dominated U.S. contingency planning in the early 1970s: a conventional war in Europe was not expected to last long enough for the reserves to make a difference. The prevailing view was that a NATO–Warsaw Pact conflict in Europe would be measured in terms of days or weeks, rather than months or years, ending early either in negotiations or in escalation to nuclear war. Nonetheless, Laird's successor, James R. Schlesinger, reminded the services of the importance of their reserve components: "Total force is no longer a 'concept.' It is now the Total Force Policy which integrates the Active, Guard, and Reserve forces into a homogeneous whole."[17] That this may have been more of a political gesture to bolster the sagging morale of the reserve community than a strong conviction of the new secretary was soon to be demonstrated.

16. Crossland and Currie, *Twice the Citizen*, p. 224. For a fuller discussion of the reorganization and its implications, see ibid., pp. 222–30.

17. Memorandum from Secretary of Defense James R. Schlesinger to Secretaries of Military Departments and others, "Readiness of the Selected Reserve," August 23, 1973.

The "Tooth-to-Tail" Factor

The thirteen-division Army was compelled to assign more responsibilities to the reserves, both to complement its diminished combat strength and to augment its support forces. Under contingency planning then in effect, the reserves would have been tapped in the early days of an emergency to supply individual fillers—ostensibly members of the Individual Ready Reserve—to bring active units up to full wartime manning levels. Planners also presumed that "high priority National Guard and Reserve divisions would achieve sufficiently high standards of combat readiness so that we could deploy them almost as rapidly as our active Army divisions."[18] The demands placed on reserve support units, on the other hand, were less imposing. Since a thirteen-division Army with 800,000 soldiers should have been able to support itself for six months of combat, reserve support units would have had ample time to be mobilized and deployed.

The role of the reserves, especially the deployment capabilities assumed for their combat and support units, was altered considerably by events in the mid-1970s. The Army, never comfortable with the thirteen-division force, convinced the Ford administration to restore the pre-Vietnam level of sixteen active divisions. This change was based partly on the view that the assumptions underlying the thirteen-division force, especially those about reserve deployability, were flawed. In 1975 Secretary of Defense James Schlesinger, who just two years earlier had emphasized the importance of the Total Force policy, concluded "that such heavy reliance on the Guard and Reserve divisions for initial defense missions would be imprudent. . . . If we are to act responsibly toward the National Guard and Reserve, we should stop pretending that we can use all of them as full substitutes for active-duty ground forces."[19]

18. *Department of Defense Annual Report to the Congress, Fiscal Years 1976 and 197T*, p. III-14.

19. Ibid. In hearings before Congress, Pentagon officials estimated that the eight National Guard combat divisions would not have been ready for deployment for at least fourteen weeks after a mobilization order. The delay was broken down as follows: alert—one week; movement to mobilization station—one week; training time—ten weeks; processing for overseas movement—two weeks. See *Fiscal Year 1976 and July–September 1976 Transition Period Authorization for Military Procurement, Research and Development, and Active Duty, Selected Reserve, and Civilian Personnel Strengths*, Hearings before the Senate Committee on Armed Services, 94 Cong. 1 sess. (GPO, 1975), pt. 5, p. 2563.

In short, said Schlesinger, it "is our belief that in the aftermath of Vietnam and the changeover to the all-volunteer force, we basically went too far in reducing our active-duty ground forces."[20]

The sixteen-division active force, however, was to be restored without any increase in active-duty strength, which by 1975 had dropped to 784,000 because of recruitment problems encountered during the first several years of the transition to an all-volunteer Army. To accommodate this constraint, the Army converted a number of support billets to combat positions, turning vacated support responsibilities over to the reserves. Nonetheless, the Army was still short, having created more combat units than could be filled with active-duty soldiers, so the "round-out" concept was introduced: four divisions, including the three new ones, were to be composed of two active brigades and one reserve brigade.[21] While many viewed this new intimate relationship between the Army's active and reserve components as a marriage of convenience, one observer close to the decision maintains that "it was the requirements of US national security, not manpower or fiscal constraints as some have erroneously assumed, that was the genesis of the Total Army concept." The idea behind the close association, according to this argument, was to return the Army's reserves "to the importance they enjoyed in World War I, World War II and the Korean war."[22]

The active Army's support forces were further squeezed by the Nunn amendment to the Defense Department Appropriation Authorization Act of 1975, which required cutting 18,000 military support positions in Europe during fiscal 1975–76 while permitting the creation of an equal number of combat positions.[23] In response to this legislation, the Army sent two more combat brigades to Europe and moved selected support units back to the United States.[24]

Clearly the restructuring of active Army forces in the 1970s entailed important changes for the reserve components. The National Guard

20. *Department of Defense Annual Report to the Congress, Fiscal Years 1976 and 197T*, p. III-15.

21. William P. Mako, *U.S. Ground Forces and the Defense of Central Europe* (Brookings, 1983), p. 26.

22. Harry G. Summers, Jr., *On Strategy: The Vietnam War in Context* (Carlisle Barracks, Penn.: U.S. Army War College, Strategic Studies Institute, 1981), p. 113.

23. P.L. 93-365, sec. 302, 88 Stat. 399, 401 (1974).

24. *Military Posture and Department of Defense Authorization for Appropriations for Fiscal Year 1977*, Hearings before the House Committee on Armed Services, 94 Cong. 2 sess. (GPO, 1976), pt. 3, p. 131.

combat divisions were relegated to the more realistic role of late-deploying reinforcements, although the several reserve brigades and battalions assigned as round-out units were expected to deploy with their parent active divisions (and as such were to be accorded higher priorities for equipment, personnel, and training resources). The major change, however, affected those support units that had earlier been considered back-up forces, to be held in reserve during the first six months of combat operations and perhaps longer. Under the new force configuration, many reserve units were earmarked to support the $4\frac{2}{3}$ division "M-day" force already in place in Europe, thus putting them among the first units to deploy in an emergency.

The drift toward greater dependence on the reserves continued into the 1980s as the Army again created more active combat units while holding its active strength constant. By fiscal 1986 the Army had added two light infantry divisions to its active structure, bringing the total to eighteen, and had combined separate National Guard units into two extra Guard divisions. By fiscal 1989, six of the eighteen active divisions included a reserve round-out brigade, and three others relied on one or more reserve round-out battalions.[25] More significantly, as indicated in the preceding chapter, more than two-thirds of the Army's tactical support capability was in the reserves, including many units that would be needed early in a crisis.[26]

The Cost Advantage

The massive transfer of functions from the active Army to its reserve components has often been justified on the grounds of cost-effectiveness. Indeed, the dollar-and-cents undertone of the Total Force concept was set in 1971 by Secretary of Defense Melvin Laird: "Lower sustaining costs of non-active duty [reserve] forces . . . allows more force units to be provided for the same cost as an all-active force structure, or the

25. *Department of Defense Annual Report to the Congress, Fiscal Year 1990*, p. 128.

26. The Army, it should be noted, removed more support missions from the active forces than could be transferred to the reserves. Consequently, it established "phantom" units, called COMPO 4, which exist only on paper. "There the 'paper tail' languishes," writes an Army officer knowledgeable about logistics, "with neither people nor equipment and with an American public and Congress unaware of the potential dangers posed by what believers in the status quo simply call an acceptable increased risk." John M. Vann, "The Forgotten Forces," *Military Review*, vol. 67 (August 1987), p. 7.

same number of force units to be maintained at lesser cost."[27] Sixteen years later the House Committee on Armed Services emphasized its continued support of reserve forces on the same basis: "The Total Force concept has proven to be an effective method of increasing U.S. national security—and at only 40 to 70 percent of the cost of active duty personnel."[28]

The cost of operating a reserve unit in peacetime is less than that of a similar active unit for several reasons. First, reservists are part-time and thus command less pay than their full-time counterparts. Second, personnel support costs and personnel replacement costs are lower for the reserve establishment. And third, operating tempo (training days, vehicle miles, aircraft flying hours) for a reserve unit is generally lower than for a similar active unit.[29]

Differences in payroll costs between active and reserve components are illustrated in table 3-1, which shows that the pay and allowances of a mechanized infantry battalion in the Army National Guard is less than a fifth of a similarly staffed unit in the active Army. This difference derives principally from the fact that the typical reservist drills one weekend a month and spends two weeks in an active-duty training program, a total of only thirty-eight days a year. Since reservists are credited with four days' worth of assemblies for their two-day weekend drill, fully participating reservists are paid for sixty-two days a year, or about a sixth of what a full-time soldier receives.[30] In fiscal 1983, for example, the average per capita payroll cost for an active Army soldier

27. *Department of Defense Annual Report to the Congress, Fiscal Year 1972*, p. 36.

28. *National Defense Authorization Act for Fiscal Year 1988/1989*, H. Rept. 100-58, 100 Cong. 1 sess. (GPO, 1987), p. 186.

29. This discussion is limited to operating costs (military personnel and operations and maintenance appropriations categories), since investment costs, if mobilized capabilities are to be equivalent, would be about the same whether a unit were active or reserve. Peacetime costs are, of course, the relevant ones for comparing active and reserve forces, since once reserves are mobilized there should be no significant differences.

30. Weekend drills are usually conducted in multiples of four hours, called unit training assemblies (UTAS). Two such four-hour assemblies are typically performed on each of the two weekend days. A member of a reserve component earns one-thirtieth of the monthly basic pay prescribed for his grade and years of service for each four-hour weekend drill period, and for each day of annual training the reservist receives one-thirtieth of the basic pay and allowances that his active-duty counterpart with the same number of dependents would receive. Not all reservists, it should be noted, adhere to this schedule; some participate in fewer or more than forty-eight drills a year and annual training periods often exceed the standard two weeks.

Table 3-1. Average Annual Peacetime Costs for Typical Mechanized Infantry and Tank Battalions, Active Army and Army National Guard, by Cost Category
Millions of fiscal 1983 dollars

	Mechanized infantry		Tank	
Cost category	Active Army	Army National Guard	Active Army	Army National Guard
Personnel costs	**18.25**	**3.78**	**13.21**	**3.06**
Pay and allowances	11.76	2.17	8.21	1.58
Other personnel	4.74	0.32	3.28	0.23
Replacement training	1.75	1.28	1.72	1.25
Equipment-related costs	**1.88**	**0.50**	**3.13**	**0.69**
Fuel	0.06	0.04	0.14	0.04
Training ammunition	0.97	0.21	1.62	0.38
Repair parts	0.66	0.20	1.19	0.23
Other	0.19	0.05	0.18	0.04
Total unit costs	**20.13**	**4.27**	**16.33**	**3.75**

Source: John F. Schank, Susan J. Bodilly, and Richard Y. Pei, *Unit Cost Analysis: Annual Recurring Operating and Support Cost Methodology*, R-3210-RA (Santa Monica, Calif.: Rand Corp., March 1986), pp. 29, 30.

was $15,252, compared with $2,073 and $2,265 for members of the Army Reserve and Army National Guard, respectively.[31]

Reserve forces also have much lower personnel overhead costs, since reservists are ineligible for the range and depth of services (recreational, family support, medical) full-time personnel receive. For the illustrative battalions shown in table 3-1, "other personnel" costs for the National Guard battalions were only about 7 percent of those for the active battalions. Finally, replacement training costs have typically been somewhat lower for reserve units, partly because they have experienced less turnover than have active units. Moreover, many of the soldiers who move into the reserves are already trained, having come directly from the active-duty ranks. For these personnel, the reserves have no need to incur the costs associated with recruitment and training.[32]

Taken together, personnel-related costs for a reserve Army unit are four to five times less than those for an active unit of the same size and

31. John F. Schank, Susan J. Bodilly, and Richard Y. Pei, *Unit Cost Analysis: Annual Recurring Operating and Support Cost Methodology*, R-3210-RA (Santa Monica, Calif.: Rand Corp., March 1986), pp. 80–81.

32. These differences, however, have narrowed in recent years, since personnel turnover in reserve units has been on the increase. See David W. Grissmer and Sheila Nataraj Kirby, *Attrition of Nonprior-Service Reservists in the Army National Guard and Army Reserve*, R-3267-RA (Santa Monica, Calif.: Rand Corp., October 1985).

rank structure.[33] The cost advantage differs among units, depending on their complement of full-time personnel. Most reserve units include some full-time personnel—active-duty personnel, full-time reservists, or federal civilians—assigned to maintain equipment and provide administrative support. Obviously, as reserve units add full-time personnel, they lose their cost advantage vis-à-vis comparable regular units.

Differences in operational activity rates also contribute to lower reserve costs. To a large extent, the costs of operating and maintaining equipment and weapon systems depend on how much they are used. Because reserve units train less than active Army units, they consume less fuel and fewer parts, ammunition, and sundry supplies. For the illustrative combat battalions in table 3-1, for instance, the reserve-active ratios for equipment-related costs range from .22 for the tank unit to .27 for the infantry unit. Since equipment-related costs make up only a small proportion of the annual recurring costs of Army units, however, the overall cost advantage of reserve units is not greatly affected by changes in activity levels. At the extreme, if the Army National Guard unit used in the earlier illustration incurred the same equipment-related costs as its active counterpart, the total cost ratio would increase only modestly, from .21 to .28. For an equipment-intensive tank battalion, the ratio would increase more, from .23 to .38. These data support the widely held view that the annual recurring costs to operate and maintain an Army reserve unit are substantially lower than those for comparably manned and equipped active units.

Taken alone, however, cost comparisons are a weak basis for drawing conclusions about the proper mix of active and reserve forces. Unless the effectiveness of the force units is also compared, the apples-and-oranges problem arises, and relative costs have limited usefulness. In the absence of acceptable measures for comparing the relative wartime effectiveness of active and reserve units, however, costs have generally been a dominant factor in force-mix issues, leaving implicit the assump-

33. These estimates omit the costs of military retirement. The Pentagon calculates these costs on an accrual basis by applying a uniform fixed normal cost percentage to the basic pay amounts in the Military Personnel Appropriations account. For fiscal 1988 these percentages were 51.2 for active duty and 26.1 for reserve personnel. Office of the Assistant Secretary of Defense (Force Management and Personnel) and others, *Manpower Requirements Report for FY 1988* (Department of Defense, February 1987), p. VIII-15. If these costs are included, the cost advantage of the reserves widens; for the typical infantry battalion shown in table 3-1, for example, the ratio would be roughly .18 rather than .21.

tion that reserve units are close substitutes for similarly configured active units.

The Politics

The Total Force policy may have its detractors, but few can be found in Congress. On the contrary, the reserves have long benefited from pressure exerted on their behalf by legislators influenced by broad grass-roots support and a strong, well-organized lobby.

The network of reserve units has been described as a part of the "intricate and subtle political chain that laces the country, running through village council rooms, county courthouses, and state capitals to Congress and the White House."[34] The armory has long been the center of community social life in many small towns. Fifty state National Guards are able to bring political pressure to bear on members of Congress through adjutants general and governors and through the Washington-based National Guard Association. The Army Reserve, though missing the powerful state affiliation, nonetheless is ably represented on Capitol Hill by the Reserve Officers Association.[35] Congress is a receptive audience, according to a former head of the Reserve Officers Association, because there is "an armory or Reserve Training Center in every Congressional district, and that means there is money to be spent on men and equipment, fuel, and supplies in that district."[36]

The political factor in reserve affairs was especially conspicuous during the 1960s, when Congress thwarted efforts by Secretary of Defense Robert S. McNamara to merge Army Reserve and National Guard components, cut their combined strength by 60,000, and save roughly $150 million a year.[37] The frustrations of administration officials were reflected in the writings of a former White House staff member:

34. Martha Derthick, "Militia Lobby in the Missile Age—The Politics of the National Guard," in Samuel P. Huntington, ed., *Changing Patterns of Military Politics* (The Free Press of Glencoe, 1962), p. 192.

35. For detailed analyses of political influence and the Army's reserve components, see Martha Derthick, *The National Guard in Politics* (Harvard University Press, 1965); and William F. Levantrosser, *Congress and the Citizen-Soldier: Legislative Policy-making for the Federal Armed Forces Reserve* (Ohio State University Press, 1967).

36. Robert H. Spiro, Jr., quoted in Michael Ganley, "Who's Guarding the Guard and Reserve?" *Armed Forces Journal International*, May 1986, p. 66.

37. Martin Binkin, *U.S. Reserve Forces: The Problem of the Weekend Warrior* (Brookings, 1974), p. 26.

"Eco-political involvements are nowhere more clearly visible than in the status of the National Guard and Reserve programs. . . . These citizen soldiers are so solidly entrenched politically that no one in Washington dares challenge them frontally."[38]

It might seem that the reserves' political clout has diminished over the past two decades as such prominent congressional stalwarts as Senator Leverett Saltonstall and Congressmen Carl Vinson, Edward T. Hebert, and L. Mendel Rivers left the scene. But there was no evidence that the influence had waned in the early 1970s when the Total Force concept was launched. In fact, 108 members (about 20 percent) of the 93d Congress held membership in one of the reserve components, and many were members of the major committees concerned with reserve legislation.[39] Nor do the reserves appear to lack strong advocates today. Their principal champions are Congressman G. V. (Sonny) Montgomery (Mississippi-Democrat) and Senator Strom Thurmond (South Carolina-Republican). Other legislators often mentioned as "the gurus of Guard and Reserve initiatives" are Congressman Charles E. Bennett (Florida-Democrat) and Senators Ted Stevens (Alaska-Republican) and Sam Nunn (Georgia-Democrat).[40]

These members, who hold prominent positions on defense-related committees, deserve credit for many of the recent initiatives to increase reserve strength and equipment. It has not been unusual, over the years, for Congress to authorize more reserve troops than an administration requested, while denying requested increases in active manpower.[41]

Also, concerned that the reserves have not been receiving a fair share of new equipment, Congress has authorized funds, over and above the administration's budget requests, for "dedicated reserve procurement." During fiscal 1980–84, for example, more than $500 million was set aside for the Army reserves, and between fiscal 1985 and 1987, another $1.4 billion was provided.[42]

---

38. Douglass Cater, *Power in Washington: A Critical Look at Today's Struggle to Govern in the Nation's Capital* (Random House, 1964), p. 41.

39. Binkin, *U.S. Reserve Forces*, pp. 25, 26.

40. Ganley, "Who's Guarding the Guard and Reserve?" p. 64.

41. See, for example, *Authorizing Appropriations, Fiscal Year 1974, for Military Procurement, Research and Development, Active-Duty and Reserve Strength, Military Training Student Loads, and for Other Purposes*, S. Rept. 93-467, 93 Cong. 1 sess. (GPO, 1973), pp. 38–40.

42. Reserve Forces Policy Board, *Fiscal Year 1983 Readiness Assessment of the Reserve Components* (Department of Defense, Office of the Secretary of Defense, 1984),

In one of the more blatant political maneuvers on behalf of the reserves, Congressman Montgomery placed in the fiscal 1989 defense authorization bill a provision that would have protected the reserve components from any budget cuts, leaving the active forces to absorb the full brunt of congressional reductions.[43] But under criticism by the Pentagon and many fellow legislators, Montgomery backed away from the proposal: "I admit my amendment went . . . too far; it's overkill."[44]

Avoiding Another Vietnam

Finally, the changes made during the mid-1970s in the Army's force structure, levying so much more responsibility on its reserve components, have also been attributed to a desire of the Army's leadership to avoid involvement in another unpopular war by devising "a much more interrelated structure that cannot be committed to sustained combat without reserve mobilization."[45] The idea was to reestablish the concept of the citizen-soldier as a bridge between the active Army and the American people, thus reducing the risk that the Army would be politically and socially isolated in a future war.

The forced reliance on the reserves has implications for the executive branch also: "If reserves must be activated in order to sustain active forces in anything more than limited contingencies, presidents will be less inclined (and politically less able) to become involved in military actions without extensive national debate and political consensus."[46] The record leaves unclear how far these concerns, rather than the other factors discussed earlier, shaped the Army's force-mix decisions, but one participant in the process has written that Army Chief of Staff General Creighton W. Abrams "hoped this return of the army to the structure it had known throughout much of the twentieth century would

---

p. 79; *Making Continuing Appropriations for the Fiscal Year 1985, and for Other Purposes*, H. Rept. 98-1159, 98 Cong. 2 sess. (GPO, 1984), p. 355; *House Joint Resolution 465: Further Continuing Appropriations for Fiscal Year 1986*, H. Rept. 99-450, 99 Cong. 1 sess. (GPO, 1985), p. 232; and *Making Continuing Appropriations for Fiscal Year 1987*, H. Rept. 99-1005, 99 Cong. 2 sess. (GPO, 1986), p. 540.

43. George C. Wilson, "House Would Bar Troop Cuts in National Guard, Army Reserves," *Washington Post*, June 16, 1988, p. A19.

44. Quoted in ibid.

45. Summers, *On Strategy*, p. 113.

46. Lacy, "Whither the All-Volunteer Force?" p. 63.

correct one of the major deficiencies of the American involvement in the Vietnam War—the commitment of the army to sustained combat without the explicit support of the American people as expressed by their representatives in Congress."[47]

Summary

In the nearly two decades since the advent of the Total Force concept, the responsibilities assigned to the Army reserves have changed dramatically. As a result of "sitting out" the Vietnam war, they had little prestige either in their own eyes or in the view of an already-skeptical regular military establishment. Despite this setback the Army reserve components have gradually been assigned roles and missions long considered the exclusive province of the active Army. This has been a remarkable development, one hard to understand or justify in terms of logic or sound defense policy: as the reserve components became weaker, they were assigned progressively more difficult and demanding tasks.

There can be no doubt that the decision to abolish conscription ushered in the reserve reformation. Constrained by its inability to expand manpower under a voluntary system, the Army chose to add division "flags" and to farm out support functions to the reserves. Whether to field more combat divisions, according to some, or to forestall a replay of Vietnam, according to others, the reasons for the restructuring seemed less than compelling, even cynical. But robust force structure analysis has rarely been demanded by Congress, especially on issues related to the reserves, for which many powerful legislators have a strong paternal interest.

The reserves became even more important to Army contingency planning in the 1980s. Under President Reagan's blueprint for "rearming America," the Army expanded its active force structure (again without any increase in active-duty strength), stretching its manpower even thinner. The reserves were seen as a ready-made solution, both by

---

47. Harry G. Summers, Jr., "The Army after Vietnam," in Kenneth J. Hagan and William R. Roberts, eds., *Against All Enemies: Interpretations of American Military History from Colonial Times to the Present* (Westport, Conn.: Greenwood Press, 1986), p. 363. Summers was a member of the Strategic Assessment Group, set up by General Abrams to devise a legitimate role for the Army in the post-Vietnam world.

traditional congressional patrons and by many of their cost-conscious colleagues, who seemed convinced, or at least sought to convince others, that the reserves constituted a genuine bargain in national security.

By the middle of the decade, the Army's reliance on its reserve components had reached a critical point, described by the top Pentagon official for reserve affairs: "The Total Force Concept of the early 1970's is a reality in 1986, so much so that contingency plans to counter aggression in both hemispheres cannot be effectively executed without committing National Guard and Reserve forces in the *same* time frame as active forces."[48] The prominence of the reserve role in contemporary contingency planning was underscored in a Pentagon report to Congress in 1983: "If the Army had to deploy more than one active division to a conflict, it would need many Army Reserve and Guard units to support those divisions unless it chose to accept the risk of drawing down its support forces in other theaters."[49] The reality that the United States would find it difficult to mount a military operation of any significance without the help of part-time soldiers has finally aroused some concern. Depending so heavily on a strategy that has no modern precedent is a risky proposition, all the more adventurous given the political obstacles to call-up and the disappointing results of earlier mobilizations.

In all fairness, however, the past may not be prologue, because of the changes that have been made under the Total Force rubric to improve the capabilities of the reserve components and to lower the political barriers to their use. Before attempting to assess the current Army active-reserve force structure, the mobilization experience of the Army reserves will be traced and the improvements that have been instituted under the Total Force policy examined.

48. Testimony by James Webb, assistant secretary of defense for reserve affairs, quoted in Lacy, "Whither the All-Volunteer Force?" p. 44. Emphasis added.

49. Office of the Assistant Secretary of Defense (Manpower, Reserve Affairs and Logistics), "The Guard, Reserve and Active Components of the Total Force," Report to the Senate Committee on Appropriations, June 30, 1983, p. 26.

CHAPTER FOUR

LESSONS FROM THE PAST

BASED ON THE cost comparisons presented in the preceding chapter, some observers have concluded that reserve forces constitute a national security bargain. In the words of one senior reserve official, "The contribution of the Army Reserve to the Total Army mission far exceeds its cost."[1] The validity of this contention, however, has been a subject of debate.

On one side, many defense officials and legislators, especially those supporters who have long advocated a larger role for the nation's citizen-soldiers, feel that the reserves not only are up to the tasks already assigned to them but should assume even greater responsibilities in the future. On the other side are critics who contend that the reserves have been given missions that they will be unable to fulfill, that they will have trouble meeting the demanding deployment schedules imposed on them by current war plans, and that their lack of proficiency when they are deployed will pose an undue risk to the nation's security interests. In between is a school of thought holding the view that the growing dependence on the reserves carries an element of risk, but one that is necessary and acceptable.[2]

The discrepancies arise because assessments of potential military capability are inherently difficult and imprecise. Most peacetime performance measures are inadequate, and the results of field exercises— the best available surrogate for wartime performance—are not publicly available. But the critics of reserve forces clearly have history on their

1. Major General William F. Ward, chief, Army Reserve, *The Posture of the Army Reserve—FY88* (U.S. Army Reserve), p. 4.
2. For example, see the comments of General Glenn K. Otis, the commander-in-chief of the U.S. Army in Europe, in Charles D. Odorizzi and Benjamin F. Schemmer, "An Exclusive *AFJ* Interview with General Glenn K. Otis," *Armed Forces Journal International,* January 1987, p. 48.

side. Indeed, political and technical problems encountered during the full mobilization in the Second World War and during three partial mobilizations in the postwar period—for the Korean conflict in 1950, the Berlin crisis in 1961, and the *Pueblo* and Tet incidents in 1968—raise serious questions concerning the advisability of counting on reserve forces for future contingencies.

The Second World War

When war broke out on the European continent in September of 1939, the U.S. Army consisted of 187,000 regulars, about 200,000 National Guardsmen, and roughly 120,000 members of the Army Reserve (then called the Organized Reserve Corps).[3] Theoretically the Army had twelve active divisions, although only three were formally organized; the National Guard comprised eighteen divisions plus basic units for four additional divisions; and the Army Reserve listed twenty-seven divisions, but these existed only on paper. The Nazi invasion of Poland prompted modest expansion of the Army and its National Guard component, but it was not until the fall of France in June of 1940 that serious actions were taken to improve U.S. military preparedness.

The mobilization of the National Guard and the call to active duty of the Organized Reserve Corps were authorized by Congress in August 1940, and the first peacetime military draft in American history was instituted in September. Reservists and conscripts were to serve for one year; their deployment outside the Western Hemisphere or U.S. possessions was prohibited. By November, about half of the National Guard had been called to federal duty, and by March of 1941 all eighteen Guard divisions had been mobilized. Of the members of the Organized Reserve Corps, roughly half (56,000) had been called up by July 1941; the number reached 80,000 by the end of the year. In contrast to the National Guard, which was mobilized in units, the Organized Reserve assigned its soldiers to vacancies in regular Army and National Guard units.

3. The Organized Reserve Corps was renamed the Army Reserve by the Armed Forces Reserve Act of 1952, P.L. 82-476, sec. 302, 66 Stat. 481, 498 (1952). Except when noted otherwise, this section on the Second World War is based on I. Heymont and E. W. McGregor, *Review and Analysis of Recent Mobilizations and Deployments of US Army Reserve Components* (McLean, Va.: Research Analysis Corp., October 1972), chap. 2.

The mobilization was less than popular in many quarters, including the Army itself. In fact, the size of the call-up far exceeded the Army's initial recommendations: "So accustomed were the Regulars to regarding the Guard with skepticism . . . that the original plan of 1940 was for only a very limited Guard mobilization. Only when the Burke-Wadsworth bill [instituting the draft] raised questions about the inequity of conscription unaccompanied by mobilization of the Guard did the General Staff decide to call out the Guard."[4]

Apparently, many members of the Guard were unhappy with the situation as well. Although Congress had limited the period of active service to one year, the National Guard experienced unusually heavy attrition. Between July 1940 and June 1941, about 96,000 guardsmen (or roughly 40 percent of the Guard's June 1940 strength) were discharged for a variety of reasons. More than 50,000 men in the lowest three grades were allowed to quit if they had dependents, close to 5,000 were underage, about 3,700 had physical disabilities, over 4,400 held jobs considered critical to the economy, and roughly 5,300 had changed their residency.[5] In addition, reaction within a mobilized National Guard division in 1941 to news that it might be kept on duty beyond October, when many of its members were scheduled to be deactivated after serving one year, brought threats of desertion. The battle cry "Over the hill in October" and its acronym, OHIO, became some of the most widely displayed graffiti of that era, "chalked on walls of latrines, field-artillery pieces, and cars."[6]

On August 18, 1941, following a rancorous debate, Congress passed the Service Extension Act of 1941, which lifted the one-year limit on conscripts and reservists.[7] This legislation exacerbated morale problems as "the autumn of 1941 produced complaints . . . over the extension of service beyond the originally stated twelve months, over the discomforts of training camp, over the inadequacy of training or of weapons, over

4. Russell F. Weigley, *History of the United States Army,* enlarged ed. (Indiana University Press, 1984), p. 427.
5. John K. Mahon, *History of the Militia and the National Guard* (Macmillan, 1983), p. 180.
6. "This Is What the Soldiers Complain About," *Life,* August 18, 1941, p. 17.
7. P.L. 213, sec. 2, 55 Stat. 626 (1941). The House had passed its version of the bill on August 12 by the narrowest of margins—203 to 202. For a discussion of the circumstances surrounding the debate, see Mark Skinner Watson, *Chief of Staff: Prewar Plans and Preparations,* United States Army in World War II: The War Department series (Department of the Army, Historical Division, 1950), pp. 214–31.

assignment to this or that unit.''[8] In late October the Army prepared responses to a list of specific grievances, several of which specifically pertained to the reserves: (1) troop morale was reported to be low; (2) National Guardsmen had been imposed on by extending their active duty without concern for family needs; (3) selectees (draftees) had been discriminated against in National Guard units and should have been trained in Organized Reserve units instead; (4) National Guard units resented assignment to them of officers from other components; (5) National Guard officers generally outranked Organized Reserve officers; (6) Organized Reserve officers received lower travel pay; and (7) the president had vetoed a bill to provide Reserve officers with uniforms.[9]

Once the Japanese attacked Pearl Harbor, morale problems gave way to a different set of concerns: recognition of the glaring deficiencies in reservists' skills, training programs, equipment, and facilities. The superannuated reserve officer corps—22 percent of the first lieutenants in the National Guard were more than 40 years old—was woefully unprepared to assist in the task of converting a horde of civilians into soldiers, much less to lead troops into combat. The Army substituted regulars for virtually all National Guard officers above the rank of lieutenant colonel and for an extremely high percentage of those in the lower officer ranks.[10]

Most of the enlisted personnel, moreover, were newly inducted, having replaced the large number of guardsmen who had been discharged in late 1940 and early 1941. On top of this, most units were equipped with obsolescent World War I weapons and lacked adequate training time and facilities. Thus it was no surprise that observers at National Guard maneuvers in August 1940 found the units unprepared, reporting "that all troops required at least three months' basic training."[11]

Once mobilized, National Guard divisions were hampered in their attempts to achieve combat readiness by the large turnover in personnel. Guard divisions had become a primary source of individual replacements for active units and fillers to organize nondivisional units. As a result of levies made on the 30th Infantry Division, for example, its strength dropped from 12,400 to 3,000 between June and August of 1942, requiring

8. Watson, *Chief of Staff*, p. 264.
9. Summarized in ibid., pp. 265–66.
10. Heymont and McGregor, *Review and Analysis*, p. 2-8.
11. Quoted in ibid., p. 2-7.

a repetition of training cycles as new inductees were assigned as replacements.[12]

Partly because of these problems, long delays were incurred between the mobilization of National Guard divisions and their readiness to deploy overseas. These delays ranged from eleven to forty-seven months, with an average of twenty-eight months for all divisions. In all fairness, however, training problems alone did not set the deployment pace. Other factors contributed, including the availability of shipping, the rate of industrial mobilization, and the deployment strategy itself, which purposely held many divisions in the United States until 1944, when the allied invasion of Europe permitted deployments to that theater.[13]

The deficiencies that plagued the Army reserves upon their mobilization, however, were more or less forgotten by V-J Day. They certainly were not uppermost in the minds of the architects of the postwar Army, who were preoccupied with salvaging a capable standing military force out of the most rapid demobilization in U.S. history. Unhappily, the lack of attention paid to the reserves in general and to mobilization plans in particular during the late 1940s exacted a toll sooner than expected.

The Korean Conflict

The outbreak of hostilities on the Korean peninsula in June of 1950 caught the United States relatively unprepared to engage in a major land campaign. With the nuclear umbrella in place, the post–World War II Army had languished at the hands of an efficiency-minded president and a parsimonious Congress. With but ten divisions and fewer than 600,000 troops, the standing Army was unable to meet General Douglas Mac-Arthur's call for additional forces to counter the Communist invasion.

Accordingly, immediate steps were taken to expand the nation's military forces, including a partial mobilization of the reserves. Four Army National Guard divisions were activated in September of 1950 but, as was the case in 1940–41, it was to be some time before these underequipped, undermanned, and poorly trained units would be ready for combat.

12. Ibid., p. 2-8.
13. Ibid., pp. 2-8 and 2-9.

Because the Selective Service Act of 1948 permitted young men from civilian life to enlist directly into the National Guard without taking active-duty training, the Guard divisions that were mobilized in 1950 "reported with only 27 to 46 percent of their personnel MOS [military occupational specialty] qualified and with most of the youngest Guardsmen having no active duty experience except for the annual 2 weeks of active duty training."[14] Many guardsmen were pulled out of their reserve units and assigned as individuals to fill out active units. Because of the need to reconstitute the Guard units with untrained replacement personnel, two of the four activated divisions—the 40th Infantry and 45th Infantry—were rated only 40 to 45 percent combat effective seven months after their mobilization. Both divisions, nonetheless, were deployed to Japan, where they were given seven to eight months' additional unit training before entering combat in December 1951 and January 1952. The other two divisions—the 28th Infantry and 43d Infantry—deployed to Europe in November 1951, following fourteen months of training in the United States. Additional Army National Guard units were mobilized during 1951: four National Guard divisions, three regimental combat teams, and more than 700 company-size units. At the peak, 96,000 guardsmen representing 30 percent of the Army National Guard were on active duty.[15]

The mobilization of the Army's other reserve component was also plagued by problems. The Organized Reserve Corps consisted of both units and individuals, the latter predominantly veterans of the Second World War who had neither trained regularly nor been on the reserve payroll and who "had been willing to remain in the reserves for use in a major emergency when everyone was needed."[16] As it turned out, these individuals were the first reservists to be called up, a decision attributed by one observer to a strong lobbying effort by the Reserve Officers Association "to prevent the calling up of larger Reserve units."[17] In fact, however, the pressing need at the outbreak of hostilities was for individual soldiers to fill critical vacancies in the active forces and as

14. Ibid., p. 1-5.
15. Herman Boland, "The Reserves," in *Studies Prepared for the President's Commission on an All-Volunteer Armed Force*, vol. 2 (Government Printing Office, 1970), p. IV-2-12; and Martin Binkin, *U.S. Reserve Forces: The Problem of the Weekend Warrior* (Brookings, 1974), p. 40.
16. Boland, "Reserves," p. IV-2-13.
17. Arthur T. Hadley, *The Straw Giant—Triumph and Failure: America's Armed Forces* (Random House, 1986), p. 107.

early replacements for combat casualties.[18] This decision aroused a great deal of controversy, since many non-unit members of the Organized Reserve Corps criticized the inequity of activating unpaid World War II veterans with rusty military skills before mobilizing the paid, trained members of ORC units, or before conscripting the "millions of young men who had never served in the military at all."[19]

These were not isolated grumblings. The severity of the issue was identified in an internal Pentagon memorandum written in October 1950:

> There is evidence of serious deterioration in the morale of reservists—a deterioration that is progressive and is expanding at an alarming rate. Indications are prevalent that a growing attitude in a large proportion of the members of the Civilian Components is their intent to resign their commissions or terminate their enlisted status at the first opportunity. This is not because of any unwillingness to serve their country in time of war, but because the reservist finds himself unduly penalized in time of *limited* mobilization.[20]

The complaints soon stimulated the interest of Congress, and a change in recall priority was announced by Army Secretary Frank Pace, Jr., early in 1952: "The Department is limited in its ability . . . to utilize the Volunteer and Inactive Reserve in that it is the desire of Congress that paid reservists be utilized in lieu of those who have not received pay for reserve activity."[21] But much damage had already been done. Despite the many contributions by close to 400,000 Army reservists called to active duty during the period, the Korean mobilization was heavily criticized:

> The largely improvised recall of reservists revealed serious shortcomings in the pre-war management of the reserve components. Reservists were recalled to duty by military skills which had changed since World War II; the Department of Defense records on reservists were not in order or up-to-date; and men were called with little or no forewarning so that they could put their business and domestic affairs in order.[22]

Many of these problems were attributed to "the Army's neglect of its

18. Boland, "Reserves," p. IV-2-12.
19. Richard B. Crossland and James T. Currie, *Twice the Citizen: A History of the United States Army Reserve, 1908–1983* (Washington, D.C.: Office of the Chief, Army Reserve, 1984), p. 97.
20. Memorandum from Rear Admiral I. M. McQuiston to the Secretaries of the Army, Navy, and Air Force, quoted in ibid., p. 100. Emphasis added.
21. Quoted in Crossland and Currie, *Twice the Citizen*, p. 98.
22. Boland, "Reserves," p. IV-2-13.

own Organized Reserve Corps [that] had created not only inequities and injustices, but also deadly inefficiency."[23]

The Berlin Crisis

If the military establishment learned any lesson from the Korean mobilization, it should have been the need for adequate planning with special attention to preparation for *partial* mobilization. But when U.S.-Soviet relations neared a flash point over the status of Berlin in 1961 and President Kennedy ordered a partial mobilization of the reserves, it appeared that all institutional memory on the thorny issue of "paid versus unpaid" reservists had been lost. The Pentagon soon found itself in a political predicament similar in many respects to the one it had faced during the Korean conflict. Although many organized units were mobilized in the fall of 1961, including four National Guard combat divisions, one Reserve training division, and various support units, a third of all mobilized Army reservists were individuals used mainly to fill out recalled units. Many of these units had fewer than half of their authorized troops, and almost a third of those were "totally unqualified in their positions."[24] Since the shortages were mainly in technical skills, the need for experienced personnel was most urgent. "These were to be found in the unpaid pool, and despite a paid drill strength in the Army components of nearly 700,000 and a requirement for less than 115,000 to be called up, approximately one-third of the recallees were not in a paid drill status."[25]

In a reprise of the Korean call-up, discontent among reservists received widespread attention from the media and ultimately aroused the concern of Congress. Once again, individual reservists were questioning "why they were recalled when men who had never served were not being drafted."[26] This kind of self-serving attitude earned reservists the disdain, even contempt, of many regulars. But to many citizen-soldiers called to active duty, the personal and financial hardships being endured seemed inconsistent with the absence of a declared national

23. Crossland and Currie, *Twice the Citizen*, p. 102.
24. Boland, "Reserves," pp. IV-2-15 and IV-2-16. A total of 113,254 Army reservists were recalled; 38,827 were individual reservists.
25. Ibid., pp. IV-2-17.
26. Crossland and Currie, *Twice the Citizen*, p. 141.

emergency and especially with a perceived lack of purpose. "Without a visible mission to perform, and without the existence of a national emergency," an Army study group concluded, "these personnel increasingly had but one objective—to go home as soon as possible."[27]

While the grousings were being discounted by some as the exception rather than the rule, the Army was issuing to its troops *Why Me?*, a pamphlet that sought to justify the call-up of individuals and to quell the criticisms.[28] But the political issue had already been joined. Some reservists warned their congressmen that "bitterness over the way the call-up has worked will be made known at the polls in next year's [1962] congressional elections."[29] The press meanwhile was reporting instances of "booing and catcalling when President Kennedy's picture appears on the screen in newsreels at [Army] camp movies."[30]

These circumstances apparently made a deep impression on Secretary of Defense Robert S. McNamara who, upon taking office earlier in the year, had initiated a major program to upgrade U.S. conventional forces. The redesigned conventional force posture "was an imposing force, and more in balance than had been the case since the Korean war. Yet it was not a force with which McNamara could be entirely satisfied." Because the call-up of the reserves in the fall of 1961 "had produced a certain amount of discontent and, with it, a flurry of Congressional protest," the reserve system "seemingly was not as available an instrument for emergencies as McNamara had hoped. For crises of a scale that did not require a major mobilization, an alternative would have to be found."[31]

Political implications aside, significant readiness problems were evident among the Army reserve units that were activated. Despite the contention by the chief of the Army Reserve in 1960 that his organization "was at its highest state of readiness ever and was basically sound and ready to complement existing ground forces," upon activation most reserve units reported being understrength, as already mentioned, and

27. Strategic Studies Institute, *Non-Mobilization and Mobilization in the Vietnam War*, Draft Report of the Study Group (Carlisle Barracks, Penn.: U.S. Army War College, January 10, 1980), p. 6.

28. " 'Why Me?'—The Army's Reply to Reservists," *U.S. News and World Report*, January 1, 1962, p. 6.

29. "Called-Up Reserves Ask: 'Why Me?' " *U.S. News and World Report*, November 27, 1961, p. 38.

30. Ibid.

31. William W. Kaufmann, *The McNamara Strategy* (Harper and Row, 1964), p. 71.

short of vital equipment.[32] While contingency plans were based on the assumption that reserve forces would be "combat ready" within three to five months after mobilization, many received intensive training for five or six months beyond that.[33]

By December of 1961, the Army proposed demobilizing some of the reserve units that were not being used effectively, but the president and secretary of defense were reluctant to do so, presumably because it would have been difficult to explain why the units had been mobilized in the first place. Meanwhile, however, disgruntlement among reservists intensified during the spring of 1962, as reflected by several incidents described in the official historical record: "Artillerymen at Fort Bragg, NC, had boycotted their mess hall March 1-4 demanding an early release. Approximately 30 wives had demonstrated in front of the main gate of Fort Devens, Mass., calling for their husbands' release; and members of the 49th Armored Division at Fort Polk, La., had held a two-hour demonstration on March 5."[34] These continued rumblings of discontent, which had already prompted the Army chief of staff to recommend that reserve units not be deployed overseas, apparently had an influence on the president, who announced on April 12 that the reserve components were to be released in August.[35]

These problems were likened by one senior Army officer to the "Over the hill in October" episode in 1941. "The vociferous complaints of 1941 and 1961," he wrote, "are footnotes to U.S. history which have repeatedly demonstrated that the average American male has little interest in active military service unless he and most of his countrymen are thoroughly convinced that the nation is in dire danger."[36] In a postmortem examination of the 1961 mobilization, a House Armed Services subcommittee found serious deficiencies among reserve units, placing much of the blame on the Army, which allowed reserve matters to "rock and stumble along without any imaginative or aggressive effort to resolve them."[37] Of special concern to the subcommittee was that the "military departments had not prepared contingency plans which con-

32. Crossland and Currie, *Twice the Citizen*, p. 134.
33. Boland, "Reserves," p. IV-2-16.
34. Crossland and Currie, *Twice the Citizen*, pp. 144–45.
35. Ibid.
36. Lynn D. Smith, "Is Pentagon Reserve Planning Realistic?" *Army*, vol. 22 (February 1972), p. 14.
37. Quoted in Crossland and Currie, *Twice the Citizen*, p. 146.

templated a partial mobilization and hence were unable to properly select units for recall," the same problem that had marred the Korean mobilization.[38]

The Berlin crisis, it should be mentioned, marked the first use of the reserve forces as an instrument of diplomacy, in this case a demonstration of national resolve intended to prevent a war rather than to fight one. In response to the Soviet challenge over Berlin, President Kennedy had requested from Congress in July 1961 the following: $3.25 billion supplemental appropriations for the armed forces, with $1.8 billion earmarked for procurement of conventional weapons, equipment, and ammunition; an increase of 217,000 in active-duty strength; a doubling and then tripling in the size of monthly draft calls; a delay in the previously planned deactivation of B-47 strategic bombers; and the authority to mobilize up to 250,000 reservists.[39]

Kennedy's strong reaction has been widely viewed as causing a major shift in the Soviets' perception of the East-West power balance and as the turning point of the Berlin crisis.[40] "Because the Berlin Crisis did not deteriorate into a hot war and because Berlin was saved as a democratic symbol in the heart of East Germany," the official historical account of the Army Reserve concludes that "the mobilization has to be rated as a qualified success."[41] It is impossible to know how heavily the relatively small reserve mobilization embedded in a package containing other, higher-profile measures weighed in the Soviets' calculations. Had the Soviets been impressed initially by the threat of an American mobilization, however, subsequent reports of the low readiness of U.S. reserve units and widespread dissension among recalled reservists would probably have altered their view.

38. Ibid.

39. "Radio and Television Report to the American People on the Berlin Crisis, July 25, 1961," *Public Papers of the Presidents: John F. Kennedy, 1961* (GPO, 1962), pp. 535–36. While the number of reservists was not specified in Kennedy's address on July 25, the number was included in the request sent to Congress the following day. See Crossland and Currie, *Twice the Citizen*, p. 136.

40. According to one scholar, Kennedy's July 25th speech "clearly and unmistakably marked the end of the period in which Khrushchev and his associates had been able to base Soviet foreign policy on inflated claims of military superiority over, or even parity with, the West." Robert M. Slusser, *The Berlin Crisis of 1961: Soviet-American Relations and the Struggle for Power in the Kremlin, June–November 1961* (Johns Hopkins University Press, 1973), p. 88.

41. Crossland and Currie, *Twice the Citizen*, p. 147.

The Vietnam War

It was not long before the mobilization question was to surface once again, but this time in reverse. In contrast to the Korean and Berlin experiences, controversy during the early years of the growing U.S. involvement in Vietnam centered on *nonmobilization*: the failure to use the reserve forces in a situation for which they seemed to be tailor-made. The issue was joined in early 1965, when proposals were being considered to expand the American military presence in South Vietnam dramatically. In the wake of a series of defeats suffered by the military forces of South Vietnam, and following a fact-finding mission to the region, Secretary of Defense McNamara made the following recommendation to President Johnson:

> Expand promptly and substantially the U.S. military pressure against the Viet Cong in the South and maintain the military pressure against the North Vietnamese in the North while launching a vigorous effort on the political side to lay the groundwork for a favorable outcome by clarifying our objectives and establishing channels of communication. This alternative would stave off defeat in the short run and offer a good chance of producing a favorable settlement in the longer run.[42]

Specifically, McNamara proposed that the number of combat battalions be increased from fifteen to thirty-four and the number of U.S. troops be raised immediately from 75,000 to 175,000, holding out the possibility that an additional 100,000 men would be needed in early 1966. To support this deployment, the secretary called for an increase of 600,000 in the total strength of the armed forces by mid-1966, to be accomplished in part by calling up 235,000 reservists, a recommendation that McNamara indicated to the president had the concurrence of Ambassador Maxwell Taylor, Deputy Ambassador U. Alexis Johnson, Ambassador-designate Henry Cabot Lodge, General Earle G. Wheeler, General William C. Westmoreland, and Admiral U. S. Grant Sharp, Jr.[43]

Despite the seeming consensus at the time, differences of opinion among military leaders—especially with regard to reserve mobilization—were later documented. The Joint Chiefs' position was stated by their chairman, General Wheeler: "We felt that it would be desirable to have

---

42. Quoted in Lyndon Baines Johnson, *The Vantage Point: Perspectives of the Presidency, 1963–1969* (Holt, Rinehart and Winston, 1971), p. 145.

43. Ibid., p. 146.

a reserve call-up in order to make sure that the people of the US knew that we were in a war and not engaged at some two-penny military adventure. Because we didn't think it was going to prove to be a two-penny military adventure by any manner or means."[44]

For his part, however, General Westmoreland was later to characterize as "premature" McNamara's proposal to call up the reserves. In his autobiographical account, Westmoreland stated that

> although I wanted an expression of national resolve, I was conscious that without congressional legislation a Reserve call-up would be for only a year, and I knew that a year would not do the job in Vietnam without a massive, uninterrupted bombing campaign against North Vietnam, which I knew the Administration was not likely to approve. I well remembered the Reserve call-up by President Kennedy during the Berlin crisis, when strong pressures arose before one year was up, to bring the boys home, a recollection that President Johnson told me later that he shared. Provided there was an equitable draft without special exceptions for anybody but the most essential civilian workers, I believed the burden of the war could be shared by the whole spectrum of American youth over an extended period, and I was convinced that it would be a long war. A call-up of Reserves should be made only when the enemy was near defeat and more American troops could assure it.[45]

In considering McNamara's proposal, the reserve question weighed heavily on the president's mind. In his memoirs, for example, Johnson recalled his concern that the call-up of large numbers of reserves "would require a great deal of money and a huge sacrifice for the American people." He was also worried that such a move would require the declaration of a national emergency, create the image that the United States was involved in a major war, and thereby risk a more direct involvement by the major Communist powers. In fact, among the reasons Johnson was later to give for rejecting McNamara's proposal was that "we would not make threatening noises to the Chinese or the Russians by calling up reserves in large numbers."[46] Thus for the second time in five years, a U.S. president underscored the importance of the reserve forces as a political instrument. In contrast to the Berlin crisis, however, when Kennedy used the reserves as a deterrent, President Johnson withheld their use, wishing to avoid provocation.

44. Quoted in Larry Berman, *Planning a Tragedy: The Americanization of the War in Vietnam* (W. W. Norton, 1982), p. 126.

45. William C. Westmoreland, *A Soldier Reports,* bookclub ed. (Doubleday, 1976), pp. 172–73.

46. Johnson, *Vantage Point,* pp. 146–47, 149.

In place of McNamara's proposal, Johnson opted for a more ambiguous and less dramatic course of action: to "give our commanders in the field the men and supplies they say they need."[47] The military, in the meantime, had scaled down their immediate requirement to 50,000 men, one-half the original estimate, which was to be met by doubling monthly draft calls, from 17,000 to 35,000.[48]

Johnson's decision to conscript more "nonvolunteers" rather than to call up reserve "volunteers" did not end the controversy. There was widespread speculation that other motives were involved. In his widely cited account of the period, for example, David Halberstam contended that Johnson "was not about to call up the reserves, because . . . [i]t would be self-evident that we were really going to war, and that we would in fact have to pay a price. Which went against all the Administration planning: this would be a war without a price, a silent, politically invisible war."[49] Although acknowledging several other contributing factors (such as sending wrong signals to adversaries and risking his goals for the Great Society), Halberstam concluded that "the decision against the reserves was convenient, it postponed the sense of reality of war, and it perpetuated both the illusion of control and of centrism within the bureaucracy. Of moderation, of Lyndon in the center, being pushed by the military but carefully weighing the alternatives, of not giving in to the military. It also meant a delay on the realization of the scope of the war, and that was crucial."[50]

Equally credible, if less sophisticated, reasons were offered by congressional leaders close to the issue. According to one press account, some members felt that the president wanted to give his new representative to the United Nations, Arthur J. Goldberg, time and opportunity to explore a peaceful settlement. Others believed that the call-up was merely being postponed until new units could be equipped.[51] Still others

47. Ibid.
48. Crossland and Currie, *Twice the Citizen,* p. 194. As matters turned out, the number of inductions more than tripled between fiscal 1965 and 1966, from about 103,000 to roughly 340,000. See Office of the Assistant Secretary of Defense (Comptroller), *Selected Manpower Statistics* (Department of Defense, April 1973), p. 50.
49. David Halberstam, *The Best and the Brightest* (Random House, 1972), p. 593.
50. Ibid., p. 594.
51. In a backgrounder following the announcement of his decision, the president "explained that the reserves, if called, would have taken several months before they were equipped to be effective in Vietnam, so he decided to use the Airmobile Division and Battalions on Okinawa which were ready to go." See *The Pentagon Papers: The*

contended that "the President had become increasingly sensitive to the possible political effects of a reserve call-up, the assumption by United States forces of the main burden of the fighting, and a big rise in casualties."[52] Indeed, some Democratic congressmen reportedly "were beginning to get 'heavy flak' from families that would be affected by a reserve call-up." All in all, there was general satisfaction in Congress "that the President had decided to increase the draft and postpone a decision on calling up reserve units."[53] The popularity of the president's decision in Congress underscored the deeply rooted political inhibitions to mobilization, deriving from the fact that "reservists and guardsmen were better connected, better educated, more affluent, and whiter than their peers in the active forces."[54]

No words were minced in *The Pentagon Papers* regarding the influence of domestic politics:

The disapproval of the reserve call up appears to have been the President's decision and was probably based more on considerations of political feasibility. As late as the 17th of July, Deputy Secretary of Defense Vance had cabled McNamara that the President had OK'd the 34 Battalion Phase I Plan and would try to "bull" the reserve call up through Senator Stennis whom he saw as his chief obstacle on this issue. The President's decision was evidently a

Defense Department History of United States Decisionmaking on Vietnam, Senator Gravel ed. (Boston: Beacon Press, n.d.), vol. 4, p. 299.

52. E. W. Kenworthy, "Most in Congress Relieved by the President's Course," *New York Times*, July 29, 1965, p. 11.

53. Ibid., p. 1.

54. Lawrence M. Baskir and William A. Strauss, *Chance and Circumstance: The Draft, the War, and the Vietnam Generation* (Alfred A. Knopf, 1978), p. 50. Personnel statistics from that period are less than reliable, but as of fiscal 1972, the last year of the draft, only 3.7 percent and 1.5 percent of the new recruits entering the Army National Guard and Army Reserve, respectively, were black, compared with 14.8 percent for the active Army. In terms of mental aptitude, 9.5 percent and 6.0 percent of the new recruits entering the Army National Guard and Army Reserve, respectively, scored in the lowest acceptable category on the Armed Forces Qualification Test, compared with 18.8 percent for the active Army. See Martin Binkin and John D. Johnston, *All-Volunteer Armed Forces: Progress, Problems, and Prospects*, prepared for the Senate Committee on Armed Services, 93 Cong. 1 sess. (GPO, June 1973), pp. 32–33. As for educational attainment, in 1970, 54 percent of reserve enlistees were either college graduates or had some college and 94 percent were high school graduates, compared with 18 percent and 74 percent, respectively, for active-duty recruits. See James L. Lacy, "Military Manpower: The American Experience and the Enduring Debate," in Andrew J. Goodpaster, Lloyd H. Elliott, and J. Allan Hovey, Jr., eds., *Toward a Consensus on Military Service: Report of the Atlantic Council's Working Group on Military Service* (Pergamon Press, 1982), p. 39; and Martin Binkin, *America's Volunteer Military: Progress and Prospects* (Brookings, 1984), p. 8.

difficult one to make. Prior to McNamara's departure for Saigon, both he and the President had hinted at press conferences that a reserve call up and higher draft calls were a distinct possibility. This, of course, triggered the predictable response from some members of Congress in opposition to a reserve call up. Upon McNamara's return from Saigon, President Johnson waited over a week before he publicly announced his Vietnam decisions. Since Vance's cable to McNamara of the 17th of July indicated that the President had approved the 34 battalion deployment, it is probably reasonable to assume that the President spent much of the week assessing the political variables of the situation. The consensus in the press was that the announced measures were not as great a leap as had been expected and that perhaps the attitude of influential Senate Democrats had restrained Johnson from taking stronger action.[55]

Thus, while many factors helped to shape Johnson's decision, the record strongly supports the conclusion reached by two military historians: "The best historical judgment of the decision not to employ Reserve Component units—particularly the Army Reserve and the Army National Guard—in Vietnam is that Johnson had made an almost purely political decision."[56]

The 1965 decision, however, did not settle the issue. The controversy over reserve mobilization continued through 1966 and 1967 as the U.S. military commitment to Southeast Asia grew sizably; by the end of 1967, 485,000 American troops were in Vietnam. The Joint Chiefs continued to register their preference for a reserve call-up to support the growing war effort, and especially to reconstitute the depleted strategic reserve, while the administration repeatedly ignored that option, largely for the same reasons that underlay the 1965 decision.[57] If anything, "in the years from 1965 to 1968 it became even more politically difficult to consider a Reserve call-up, because the Reserve components had

55. *Pentagon Papers,* vol. 4, p. 299.

56. Crossland and Currie, *Twice the Citizen,* p. 195.

57. During consideration of build-up alternatives in 1966, McNamara reiterated the earlier theme: "The political aspects of a Reserve call-up are extremely delicate." See *Pentagon Papers,* vol. 4, p. 314. According to one account: "The JCS had attempted a half-dozen times to persuade President Johnson and Secretary McNamara to mobilize reservists and thus replenish the strategic reserves. Each time the budget was discussed and each time additional troops for Vietnam were being considered they raised the issue." John B. Henry II, "February, 1968," *Foreign Policy,* no. 4 (Fall 1971), p. 8. By one reliable account, "the resulting frustration of the chiefs over the mobilization issue was particularly severe and reached crisis proportions in the fall of 1967, when the chiefs reportedly considered resignation en masse in protest." See General Bruce Palmer, Jr., *The 25-Year War: America's Military Role in Vietnam* (University Press of Kentucky, 1984), p. 44.

become havens for those who wanted to avoid active military duty—and Vietnam.''[58]

Thus the reserve mobilization question influenced major decisions taken during the Vietnam era to a much greater extent than has been popularly supposed. One well-informed Pentagon insider at the time was later to write that

> the great debate within the administration in 1967 was over the conduct of the ground war, and that debate revolved around one crucial factor—mobilization. When the president began to search for the elusive point at which the costs of Vietnam would become unacceptable to the American people, he always settled upon mobilization, the point at which reserves would have to be called up to support a war that was becoming increasingly distasteful to the American public.[59]

The same observer contended that this constraint on the use of reserves, "with all its political and social repercussions, not any argument about strategic concepts or the 'philosophy' of the war, *dictated American war policy*."[60] While this view may seem overdrawn, it is interesting to speculate on the course of events had Johnson elected in 1965 to mobilize the reserves rather than expand the draft. This course would have required the declaration of a national emergency, which in all probability would have prompted an earlier public examination of U.S. involvement in Southeast Asia. "Such a debate," it has been concluded, "might well have revealed the painfully learned truth that there was not a deep and enduring national resolve on the question of Vietnam, and it might have foreshortened the US involvement in the war."[61]

It can be argued, too, that a mobilization of reserves in 1965 would have meant the earlier *personal* involvement of middle-class and upper-class America, which might have created greater domestic political resistance against expanding the U.S. role in Vietnam. In retrospect, the reforms of the Selective Service System that made white upper-class youths more vulnerable to the draft and the growing political agitation for ending American involvement in the war seem more than coincidental.[62]

58. Crossland and Currie, *Twice the Citizen*, p. 197.
59. Herbert Y. Schandler, *The Unmaking of a President: Lyndon Johnson and Vietnam* (Princeton University Press, 1977), p. 56.
60. Ibid. Emphasis added.
61. Crossland and Currie, *Twice the Citizen*, p. 209.
62. Among the changes to the Selective Service System were a random lottery to replace draft board decisions and an end to student, occupational, and fatherhood deferments.

Two events in January 1968—the capture of the USS *Pueblo* by the North Koreans and the beginning of the Tet offensive in Vietnam— created a situation in which proponents of reserve mobilization finally prevailed. Even then, only a modest number of reservists were activated and, as in previous call-ups, the results were less than satisfying.

The first call-up was announced on January 25, 1968, two days after the North Koreans seized the U.S. intelligence ship *Pueblo*. Amid signs that the South Koreans, fearful of an invasion from the north, might withdraw their forces from Vietnam, President Johnson decided to call up more than 14,000 Air Force and Navy reserves.[63] Ten tactical fighter and four tactical reconnaissance units from the Air National Guard were mobilized, along with seven military airlift and one aerospace rescue and recovery unit from the Air Force Reserve. In addition six Naval Air Reserve fighter squadrons were activated.[64] Although Johnson later stated that the call-up was intended "to strengthen our position in Korea without diverting resources from Southeast Asia,"[65] there was press speculation that the president was also flashing a signal of U.S. resolve. The Associated Press reported that "the call-up is generally viewed as an administration effort to put some military bite behind the diplomatic bark directed at the North Koreans," while United Press viewed the action "as a diplomatic signal in itself, directed as much to Moscow as Pyongyang, that the United States means what it says in demanding the return of the *Pueblo*."[66] The *Wall Street Journal,* meanwhile, speculated that the call-up might have been "a rather roundabout way to get more troops for the Vietnam war."[67] Whether the call-up was meant mainly as a diplomatic signal and, if it was, how well it succeeded remain debatable.[68] What is evident, however, is that the call-up had little effect

63. Johnson, *Vantage Point,* p. 385.
64. *Annual Report of the Secretary of Defense on Reserve Forces, Fiscal Year 1968,* pp. 65, 81, 103.
65. Johnson, *Vantage Point,* p. 385.
66. Wire service stories quoted in John D. Williams, "Public Affairs Aspects of the 1968 Reserve Mobilization," *Air University Review,* vol. 23 (November–December 1971), p. 61.
67. Norman Sklarewitz, "Where Are They Now? Activated Reserves Just Waiting Around," *Wall Street Journal,* March 15, 1968, p. 1.
68. These questions are always difficult to sort out. Analysts have speculated that U.S. objectives were threefold: (1) to deter the North Koreans from again using force; (2) to induce the South Koreans to maintain their military presence in South Vietnam; and (3) to deter the Soviet Union from spurring undesirable behavior by North Korea. One analysis concludes that the latter two objectives were satisfied but the first was

on the North Vietnamese, who launched their Tet offensive on January 31st—the Asian New Year holiday—just six days after the reserve mobilization announcement.

The stunning Tet offensive of 1968, viewed as a military failure but a psychological success for the enemy and as a major turning point in the Vietnam war, caused the administration to undertake an A-to-Z reassessment of the objectives and purposes of American involvement and, in so doing, thrust to the fore once again the issue of reserve mobilization. Within two weeks of the beginning of the Tet operation, General Westmoreland requested and was granted about 10,000 troops over and above the 525,000 already in-country or earmarked for assignment.[69] General Wheeler again raised the subject of reserve mobilization, but Secretary McNamara was opposed. The president, for his part, remembering "the complaints about the call-up of reserves during President Kennedy's administration and, more recently, the failure to use effectively those who had been called up during the *Pueblo* crisis," asked for further study of the problem.[70]

The issue of a larger call-up came to a head in late February of 1968, when Generals Wheeler and Westmoreland raised the stakes by proposing that another 206,000 Army troops be provided; 108,000 were to be deployed to Vietnam by May 1, 1968, and the remainder were to be kept in the strategic reserves, to be made available for Vietnam "if all the worst contingencies materialized."[71] That proposal would have meant increasing total military strength by roughly 400,000 troops, a prospect that virtually all participants agreed would require the long-avoided mobilization.[72] By the Pentagon's reckoning, 260,000 reservists would

---

not, given the incident in the following year in which the North Koreans shot down a U.S. EC-121 aircraft. See Barry M. Blechman and Stephen S. Kaplan, *Force without War: U.S. Armed Forces as a Political Instrument* (Brookings, 1978), p. 81.

69. Johnson, *Vantage Point*, p. 386.

70. Ibid., pp. 386–87.

71. Henry, "February, 1968," pp. 16–17.

72. As mentioned earlier, General Westmoreland opposed a reserve call-up in 1965–66; he now favored mobilization, explaining that "I was in much the same position as any battlefield commander at whatever level who must choose the optimum time to influence the battle by committing his reserve force; the enemy's losses in the Tet offensive had at last presented the right opportunity. I was convinced that with additional strength and removal of the old restrictive policy, we could deal telling blows—physically and psychologically—well within the time frame of the reservists' one-year tour. The time had come to prepare and commit the Reserve." See Westmoreland, *A Soldier Reports*, p. 430.

have to be activated, a figure that was soon revised downward to 98,000.[73] By March 22d, the estimate had been scaled down even further; only 13,500 additional troops would be sent to Vietnam and 62,000 reservists would be called up.[74] As matters turned out, however, just under 20,500 reservists were ordered to active duty in May 1968, joining the naval and air force units that had been activated in January.[75] Apparently the final call-up number had been further cut for budgetary reasons.[76]

It is ironic that the relatively small reserve activations of 1968, coming as they did after several years' debate and ample opportunity for contingency planning, and with the lessons of earlier mobilizations well documented, were laden with difficulties. The January call-up of Navy and Air Force reserve units was tainted by press reports critical of the preparedness of the reservists: "Some military officials also say it's a good thing the reserves haven't been sent to Vietnam or Korea. They say the men just aren't prepared to fight."[77] These reports were soon followed by widespread media coverage of complaints among mobilized reservists, some of whom "charged that they had been rushed to active duty but now found themselves with little to do." Others took exception to being recruited by the "Train with your buddies, serve with your buddies" theme and then being reassigned as individuals out of their reserve unit.[78]

Attempting to defuse the complaints about inactivity, the Pentagon explained that "although the reserve units were mobilized because of the *Pueblo* incident, they were not necessarily called to active duty to serve only in Korea. . . . [N]ow that they are on active duty, they [are] a portion of the total world-wide defense structure." As for the "unit integrity" issue, Defense officials cited a standing 1959 directive that personnel would be ordered to active duty only with their units, but their subsequent reassignment was not prohibited.[79] These media accounts aroused the concern of several powerful members of Congress, whose

73. Johnson, *Vantage Point*, pp. 391, 407.

74. Ibid., p. 415. Reportedly the president asked General Wheeler to advise General Westmoreland that "a major call-up of Reserves . . . was politically infeasible." See Westmoreland, *A Soldier Reports*, p. 436.

75. *Annual Report of the Secretary of Defense on Reserve Forces, Fiscal Year 1968*, p. C-2. Besides the reservists assigned to units, 1,692 Army Individual Ready Reservists were called to active duty.

76. Crossland and Currie, *Twice the Citizen*, p. 202.

77. Sklarewitz, "Where Are They Now?" p. 1.

78. Williams, "Public Affairs Aspects of the 1968 Reserve Mobilization," pp. 61, 64.

79. Ibid., pp. 63, 65.

protests led to changes in Army assignment policies and, as noted above, gave President Johnson pause when considering the Army call-up several months later.

The president was right to worry. Indeed, the difficulties that marked the January 1968 call-up of naval and air reserve units were modest in comparison with those surrounding the mobilization of Army reserve units in May 1968. In that instance, the problems went beyond complaints of inactivity and breach of unit integrity to serious questions concerning the state of readiness of the activated units. Army planners had assumed that the units slated for activation would be "combat ready." In the event, every one of the seventy-six Army Reserve and Guard units failed to meet that readiness standard. As for equipment, all units were rated C-4—not combat ready.[80] In other words, *every* unit was deficient either in the amount or in the condition of its authorized equipment.

The personnel situation was not much better: 49 percent of unit personnel were not fully trained or qualified, and 17 percent were totally unqualified for their assigned positions.[81] This situation contributed to lengthy delays in achieving combat readiness, since individual skill training had to be conducted concurrently with normal unit training. Thirty-five units of the Army Reserve were eventually deployed to Vietnam, but only after six or seven months of training in some cases.[82] Similar problems affected the National Guard. Two brigades had been activated. One did not achieve combat readiness until some seven months after mobilization and was demobilized in December 1969. The other brigade did not complete battalion training tests until fifteen weeks after mobilization. It was reorganized in early 1969 and replaced a brigade in the 5th Infantry Division that had been sent to Vietnam.[83]

These problems resulted largely from inadequate planning and faulty execution. Although a contingency plan for partial mobilization had been on file since 1962, the Army saw no need to keep it current after the 1965 decision. Thus formal planning for the 1968 call-up did not begin until after the *Pueblo* incident when, in a rush of activity, about seventy-five alternatives were devised over an eleven-week period.[84] The fact that the Army reserve components were in the middle of a substantial

80. John D. Stuckey and Joseph H. Pistorius, "Mobilization for the Vietnam War: A Political and Military Catastrophe," *Parameters*, vol. 15 (Spring 1985), p. 35.

81. Boland, "Reserves," pp. IV-2-22, IV-2-23.

82. Crossland and Currie, *Twice the Citizen*, p. 207.

83. Heymont and McGregor, *Review and Analysis*, pp. 5-12, 5-15.

84. Stuckey and Pistorius, "Mobilization for the Vietnam War," p. 32.

reorganization did not help the situation. Moreover, the readiness status of reserve units was virtually unknown, since "the readiness reporting system of reserve components had been suspended by the Undersecretary of the Army in 1966." The pace of activity was hectic: "Revisions in lists of selected units occurred almost daily. There was no coordination in developing troop lists between the full Army staff, CONARC [Continental Army Command] headquarters, the Continental US Armies, State Adjutants General, or Reserve Commands."[85]

The final selection of the Army reserve units to be called up was made by the assistant chief of staff for force development in "frantic consultation" with the respective heads of the National Guard Bureau and the Army Reserve.[86] Political and bureaucratic compromises were evident in the final list. Readiness considerations gave way to concerns that recalled units should be geographically representative (seventy-six units represented thirty-four states), that the contributions by the Army National Guard and Reserve components would be proportional, and that every state would be left with enough capability to handle civil disturbances. By these criteria, some units selected for call-up were manned and equipped at levels lower than similar reserve units that were not mobilized.[87]

In retrospect, this mobilization took place under what should have been "ideal" conditions. Mobilized units were battalion-size or smaller. The time for planning before call-up was more than adequate, and active Army posts were well prepared to receive the units. The on-going draft was available to supply fillers. Perhaps more important, the number called was small enough so that the best units could be selected. Why, then, were the results so unsatisfactory? One possible answer was to be found in the institutional tensions between the regular Army and its reserve components: "The mobilization itself, once ordered by the Commander in Chief, was conducted by OSD [Office of the Secretary of Defense] and HQDA [Headquarters, Department of the Army] in a manner of gross ineptitude: the preparation for a mobilization was impudently unsuitable; the conduct of the mobilization was contemptuous; the demobilization was a comedy of errors. And once the forces were mobilized, countless problems were inflicted by the Regular Army—as

85. Ibid.
86. Ibid., p. 34.
87. Ibid.

has been true throughout U.S. history.''[88] This evaluation reflects the deep feelings that have traditionally marked relations between the Army's active and reserve factions, a natural cleavage between professional and citizen soldiers that widens in the face of a shrinking availability of defense resources or a growing perception that reserve forces are substitutes for—rather than complements to—the active forces.

Conclusions

The main characteristics of the four mobilization experiences discussed above are summarized in table 4-1. The World War II mobilization stands apart from the other three, both because it was total rather than partial, and because it preceded hostilities by a prolonged period. Also note that each of the four mobilizations involved successively smaller numbers of reservists and reserve units. This shrinkage was due, not to successively smaller threats, but rather to increasing loss of confidence in the readiness of the reserves (based on their earlier mobilization performance) and to increasing political inhibitions.

On balance, the nation's experience with mobilizing its reserve forces has been disappointing. Whatever beneficial purposes have been served by the call-ups of Army reserve units in the past, they have been accompanied by numerous problems, including widespread confusion about recall priorities, general unpreparedness of mobilized units, prolonged delays between the mobilization of Guard and Reserve units and their deployments, frequent instances of unwillingness to serve, and in some cases the ineffective use of those units. While many lessons can be drawn from these experiences, several in particular stand out.

First and foremost is that history is relevant, and officials responsible for shaping the nation's mobilization policies should have studied it. Instead, avoidable mistakes were repeated by several generations of decisionmakers and planners, who share some of the responsibilities for the poor showing of the Army reserves since the Second World War.

Second, contrary to theoretical peacetime planning that the National Guard and Reserve would be mobilized and deployed as integral units, this has not been the case in practice, especially for combat organizations. Once called up, reserve units have been used as an immediate source of

88. Ibid., p. 37.

Table 4-1. Selected Features of Army Reserve Mobilizations since World War II

Features	World War II		Korea	
Scope	M-day = D-day − 15 months; total mobilization; major deployments		M-day = D-day; partial mobilization; major deployments	
Premobilization situation				
Regular army	3 divisions, 185,000 troops		10 divisions, 590,000 troops	
Reserve components	**Army Reserve**	**National Guard**	**Army Reserve**	**National Guard**
Basic force structure	27 divisions	18 divisions	25 divisions	27 divisions
Personnel strength	120,000	200,000	600,000	325,000
Unit training (annual)[b]	Limited	48 paid drills	Paid drills	48 paid drills
Facilities	None	Inadequate	Inadequate	Inadequate
Materiel	None	Extreme shortages	Extreme shortages	46 percent of TOE[c]
Mobilization situation				
Units mobilized	None	18 divisions and 136 other units	971 company-size units	8 divisions and other small units
Personnel mobilized	136,000	297,754	241,500	138,500
Percent TOE strength[c]	. . .	41–56[e]	Mostly individuals	34–55[e]
Percent MOS-qualified[f]	n.a.	n.a.	Mostly experienced veterans	27–46
Facilities	. . .	Inadequate initially	Inadequate initially	Inadequate initially
Materiel	. . .	Totally inadequate	Limited	35 percent of TOE[c]
Postmobilization situation				
Personnel				
Fill requirement	. . .	197,530	. . .	96,160
Time to fill	. . .	7 months[e]	. . .	2 months[e]
Training (divisional)				
Requirement (weeks)	. . .	44 (later 32)	. . .	28
Completion (weeks)	. . .	Average 120	. . .	32–35
Materiel	. . .	Adequate by 1943	. . .	Improvement during unit training

Source: I. Heymont and E. W. McGregor, *Review and Analysis of Recent Mobilizations and Deployments of US Army Reserve Components* (McLean, Va.; Research Analysis Corp., October 1972), pp. 1-2, 4-3.

n.a. Not available.

a. Units include thirteen training divisions in 1961 and 1968, and three separate infantry brigades in 1968.

b. Paid drills before Vietnam were two hours weekly; during the Vietnam buildup, drills were increased to four hours and multiple drills were conducted on weekends. In addition, during the Vietnam era 150,000 reservists in the Selected Reserve Force (SRF) were authorized seventy-two drill periods, reduced to fifty-eight in 1967.

c. TOE is the acronym for Table of Organization and Equipment, which sets out the authorized numbers of personnel and major equipment in a unit or formation.

Table 4-1 *(Continued)*

Berlin, 1961		Vietnam, 1968	
No hostilities; small partial mobilization; no major deployments		M-day = D-day + 36 months; extremely small partial mobilization; no major deployments	
14 divisions, 860,000 troops		18⅔ divisions, 1,500,000 troops	
Army Reserve	**National Guard**	**Army Reserve**	**National Guard**
10 divisions (4,398 units)[a]	27 divisions (4,497 units)	3,482 units[a]	8 divisions (3,034 units)
1,900,000	394,000	1,217,984	411,419
48 paid drills	48 paid drills	48 paid drills	48 paid drills
Inadequate	Inadequate	Inadequate for unit training	Inadequate for unit training
Obsolescent; shortages of essential equipment	Critical shortages	Inadequate	Inadequate
1 training division (441 company-size units)	2 divisions, 1 ACR[d], and others (446 company-size units)	1 infantry battalion and 41 other units	2 infantry brigades and other small units
68,813 (30,056 in units)	44,371	7,953	12,234
67	62–69[e]	82	89
67	67	85	85
Adequate	Adequate	Adequate	Adequate
Major shortages	50 percent of TOE[c]	REDCON C-4[g]	REDCON C-4[g]
15,234	9,830	698	1,512
2 months	3 months[e]	Up to 5 months	Up to 5 months
Varied	27 compressed to 13[e]	7–8	15
Required full unit ATP[h]	13[e]	7–15	15–17
Continued shortages	60 percent within 3 months[e]	REDCON C-1 within 60 days[g]	REDCON C-1 within 60 days[g]

d. ACR—armored cavalry regiment.

e. Applied to divisions but representative of all units.

f. MOS—military occupational specialty.

g. REDCON, or readiness condition, is a system (now called Unit Status and Identification Report, or UNITREP) designed to measure the readiness of military units. Ratings range from C-1 (fully ready) to C-4 (not ready), based on such things as the availability of personnel and equipment, the condition of equipment, and the status of personnel training.

h. ATP—annual training period.

trained junior enlisted replacements and fillers subject to levies by the active Army. In fact, not since the Second World War has a National Guard division been deployed with its original complement of personnel. Stripped of most of their personnel, the divisions that have been mobilized have had to be reconstituted and trained before they could be deployed.

Third, the record shows domestic politics have strongly influenced decisions concerning the use of reserve forces. The most salient example was President Johnson's determination in 1965 to rely on the draft rather than on the reserves to expand U.S. involvement in Vietnam. That decision cast a stigma on the reserve forces that is yet to be completely erased. Indeed, there remains today deep concern about the wisdom of adopting a military strategy that depends, in the final analysis, on a presidential decision to mobilize reserve forces. Moreover, in those instances when the reserves have been mobilized, domestic politics has played a disruptive role in the selection of units to be activated and in the timing of their demobilization.

Fourth, serious rivalries have existed between the regular military establishment and its reserve counterpart. While many factors have contributed to the general unpreparedness of the reserve units that have been mobilized in the past, much of the blame must be attributed to a neglect of the reserves in Pentagon planning, programming, and budgeting, processes that have been controlled largely by active-duty military officers.

Fifth, the use of reserve forces as an instrument of diplomacy has had important limitations as well as advantages. As demonstrated during the Berlin and *Pueblo* crises, the idleness that has afflicted reserve forces mobilized as symbols of political resolve has reduced the morale and hence the effectiveness of the reservists. By contrast, fewer problems have been reported in units that have been mobilized for genuine emergencies or have been actively involved in fulfilling meaningful military missions.

Finally, *partial* call-ups have presented challenging personnel management problems. Short of general mobilization (as in the Second World War), the question of "who serves when not all serve?" has invariably surfaced. The call-up of individual reservists has repeatedly elicited strong criticism, especially when they have been activated before their colleagues serving in units—soldiers who are, after all, not only better trained but also paid to maintain their preparedness.

CHAPTER FIVE

REVITALIZING THE RESERVES, 1971–88

IF HISTORY is any guide, the contemporary Army's unprecedented dependence on the reserves is a risky venture. Defense planners are heavily basing the nation's security on the expectation that today's Army reserve units will be able to accomplish what few of their predecessors were able to do—go to war on short notice.

Still, many changes have been made since the disappointing Vietnam experience. Congress and the military establishment have improved the capabilities of the Army reserves and refined their call-up procedures. Specifically, equipment shortages have been reduced, more individual and unit training conducted, closer ties to the active forces forged, and more discretionary call-up authority given to the president.

As discussed in chapter 3, the tandem decisions in the early 1970s to reduce the size of the post-Vietnam standing Army and end the draft gave rise to the concept of Total Force planning: using *all* appropriate resources—both U.S. and free world—to capitalize on the potential of available assets. For U.S. military forces, this policy has meant concurrent consideration of total forces, active and reserves, to determine the most advantageous mix to support national strategy. As explained by Secretary of Defense Melvin R. Laird, the principal architect of the strategy:

> Members of the National Guard and Reserve, instead of draftees, will be the initial and primary source for augmentation of the active forces in any future emergency requiring a rapid and substantial expansion of the active forces. . . . [This] requires that the capability and mobilization readiness of Guard and Reserve units be promptly and effectively enhanced. We are taking steps to do so.[1]

In light of the unpreparedness of the Army reserve forces at the time,

1. *Department of Defense Annual Report to the Congress, Fiscal Year 1972*, p. 36.

attaining a respectable state of readiness posed a formidable challenge. During the 1960s reserve units had been stripped of essential equipment, they were virtually bereft of usable training facilities, and while their ranks were filled, many of their members were draft-averse "volunteers" seeking to avoid combat duty in Vietnam. In short, by the close of the decade the Army Reserve's warfighting ability was at its nadir.[2]

If they were to become full-fledged partners with the active forces, as the Total Force pronouncements indicated, the reserves would have to be manned, trained, and equipped to levels unprecedented in their history. And if the problems that plagued past mobilizations were to be avoided, the Pentagon would have to develop plans for an effective call-up, with special attention to its political aspects. Were these goals met?

Manning the Reserves

At the beginning of the 1970s the Army reserve components were at full strength. In fact, thanks to the draft, the reserve rolls were bulging and a seemingly endless queue of applicants had formed. Moreover, since the reserve components could pick and choose among those applicants, the quality of their membership, as measured by level of education and aptitude test scores, was much higher than in the active forces at the time. In addition, the Individual Ready Reserve was heading toward the one million mark as the large pool of Vietnam-era conscripts completed their active service and transferred to the reserves to fulfill their six-year service obligation.

Paradoxically, this large collection of bright, educated reservists represented little military capability. Most of the draft-induced volunteers were merely "counting the days," but even motivated reservists found it hard to qualify in their designated skills because they lacked equipment and adequate training facilities. According to one participant: "Reserve commanders were forced to turn to movies and classroom lectures to fill inactive duty training time. It was quite common for NCOs to read lesson plans to masses of sleepy, bored, college-educated first-termers while the officers and full-time technicians wrestled with admin-

2. Richard B. Crossland and James T. Currie, *Twice the Citizen: A History of the United States Army Reserve, 1908–1983* (Washington, D.C.: Office of the Chief, Army Reserve, 1984), pp. 211–12.

Figure 5-1. Army Personnel, by Component, Fiscal Years 1972–89ᵃ

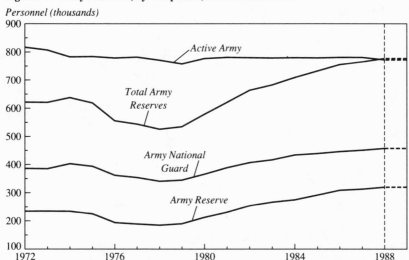

Personnel (thousands)

Sources: National Guard and Reserve data for fiscal 1972–76 reserve from Office of the Assistant Secretary of Defense (Manpower, Reserve Affairs and Logistics), *Manpower Requirements Report for FY 1979* (Department of Defense, February 1978), p. IX-14. National Guard and Reserve data for fiscal 1977–87 and active Army data for fiscal 1972–87 from Directorate for Information Operations and Reports, Washington Headquarters Services, *Selected Manpower Statistics, Fiscal Year 1987,* DIOR/MO1-87 (Department of Defense), pp. 204 and 68, respectively. Projections for fiscal 1988–89 from Office of the Assistant Secretary of Defense (Force Management and Personnel) and others, *Manpower Requirements Report for FY 1989* (Department of Defense, March 1988), p. II-4.

a. Data for Army National Guard and Army Reserve include only those in the Selected Reserve. Trends for 1988–89 are projected.

istration."[3] The Individual Ready Reserve, too, was largely a paper organization, as little effort was made to keep the roster current, and it was doubtful if many on the rolls would have shown up on a timely basis or, indeed, would have shown up at all.[4]

Trends in Reserve Manning

Since the advent of the Total Force concept and the end of conscription, manning in the Army reserve components has undergone significant changes. For the first several years (1972–75), the strength of both the Army National Guard and the Army Reserve remained reasonably stable (see figure 5-1), but the academic and aptitude credentials of new recruits

3. Ibid., p. 233.
4. See, for example, *Defense Manpower Commission Staff Studies and Supporting Papers,* vol. 2: *The Total Force and Its Manpower Requirements Including Overviews of Each Service* (Government Printing Office, 1976), p. H-13.

Figure 5-2. Percentage of Army Recruits with High School Diplomas, by Component, Fiscal Years 1972–87[a]

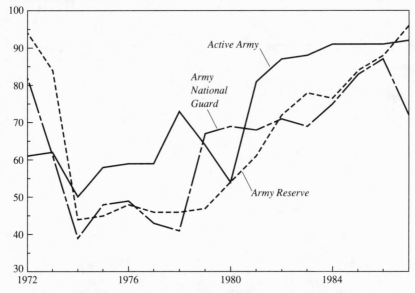

Sources: Active Army data for fiscal 1972–77 from Office of the Assistant Secretary of Defense (Manpower, Reserve Affairs and Logistics), *America's Volunteers: A Report on the All-Volunteer Armed Forces* (Department of Defense, 1978), p. 199; and fiscal 1978–87 data obtained from Defense Manpower Data Center. Guard and Reserve data for fiscal 1972–76 adapted from *Military Posture and Department of Defense Authorization for Appropriations for Fiscal Year 1978,* Hearings before the House Committee on Armed Services, 95 Cong. 1 sess. (Government Printing Office, 1977), pt. 5, p. 1183; fiscal 1977–79 data from Department of Defense unpublished data: and fiscal 1980–87 data adapted from Assistant Secretary of Defense (Reserve Affairs), *Official Guard and Reserve Manpower Strengths and Statistics* (Department of Defense), report G7, selected years.

a. Guard and Reserve data include only those in the Selected Reserve; fiscal 1972–76 reserve data are for males only. Guard and Reserve data, especially for the earlier years, are unreliable and should be interpreted with caution. Even recent reserve data are inconsistent with active Army figures, since the former count high school seniors and those with high school equivalency as graduates. Moreover, different sources in the Pentagon provide widely different data; for example, much higher fiscal 1980–86 percentages for the reserves can be found in *Department of Defense Appropriations for 1988,* Hearings before the Subcommittee on the Department of Defense of the House Committee on Appropriations, 100 Cong. 1 sess. (GPO, 1987), pt. 3, p. 9.

plummeted.[5] For example, recruits with high school diplomas fell from 82 to 48 percent for the Army National Guard and from 95 to 45 percent for the Army Reserve (figure 5-2). Furthermore the percentage of new entrants with test scores in the lowest acceptable category shot up, from under 10 percent to approximately 25 percent for both components

---

5. By convention, the concept of "quality" has been described in easy-to-measure terms of educational level and standardized test scores. The "choice" recruit has a high school diploma and an above-average score on the Armed Forces Qualification Test (AFQT). For a further description, see Martin Binkin, *Military Technology and Defense Manpower* (Brookings, 1986), pp. 3–22.

Figure 5-3. Percentage of Army Recruits with Below-Average Aptitude, by Component, Fiscal Years 1972–87[a]

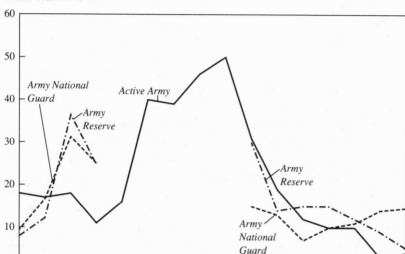

Sources: Active Army data for fiscal 1972–75 from *America's Volunteers*, p. 197; and fiscal 1976–87 data obtained from Defense Manpower Data Center. Guard and Reserve data for fiscal 1972–75 adapted from *Military Posture*, p. 1189; fiscal 1981–86 data provided by the Office of the Assistant Secretary of Defense (Force Management and Personnel); and fiscal 1987 data adapted from Assistant Secretary of Defense (Reserve Affairs), *Official Guard and Reserve Manpower Strengths and Statistics, FY 1987 Summary* (Department of Defense, 1987), pp. 232–33. (Note that the latter's figures on test scores are not considered reliable for the early 1980s.)

a. Guard and Reserve data include only those in the Selected Reserve. Guard and Reserve data for fiscal 1972–75 are for males only. As explained in the text, reliable data for the Guard and Reserve are not available for fiscal 1976–80.

(figure 5-3).[6] Both the National Guard and the Reserve, mirroring the active Army's experience during the transition to an all-volunteer force, accepted larger numbers of women and minorities and, to reduce their need for new recruits, made greater efforts to attract veterans leaving active duty. In contrast to fiscal 1971, for example, when roughly 80 percent of all new entrants to both Army reserve components were recruited from the civilian population, by fiscal 1974 the proportions had

6. All recruits take the AFQT, a composite that includes word knowledge, arithmetic reasoning, paragraph comprehension, and numerical operations. On the basis of his or her score, which is viewed as an index of general trainability, an examinee is placed in one of five groups: AFQT category I, percentile score 93–99; category II, 65–92; category III, 31–64; category IV, 10–30; and category V, 9 and below. The military services prefer to recruit people from the top three categories, since entrants scoring below the 31st percentile have been found to require more training and present greater disciplinary problems. Those in category V, below the 10th percentile, are disqualified. For further discussion, see ibid., pp. 13–22.

dropped to 27 percent for the National Guard and to only 17 percent for the Reserves.[7]

Planners had anticipated some decline in the quality of reserve recruits with the end of conscription, but the sharpness of the drop was surprising. Two reasons stand out: the reserves lacked a recruiting apparatus, and they were unfamiliar with the use of recruitment incentives. Also, a general disinterest on the part of the active Army, which was grappling with recruitment problems of its own, contributed to the decline.

Because the reserves were not able to recruit and retain enough volunteers to maintain their strength, Congress reduced Army reserve manpower authorizations in the later 1970s. In 1977 the incoming Carter administration optimistically raised the Army Reserve strength goal to 225,000, to be attained by fiscal 1979. In spite of that goal, before the end of the decade the Army Reserve had dropped to less than 186,000 and the Army Guard to just under 341,000, for a combined shortfall of about 133,000 as measured against peacetime manning objectives.[8] In addition, the reserves still found it hard to attract high school graduates and, by all indications, new recruits' entry test scores dropped as well.[9]

This downward trend for the reserves mirrored the troubles of the active Army, whose personnel quality reached postwar lows during the same period.[10] The underlying causes of the reserves' recruitment

7. *Military Posture and Department of Defense Authorization for Appropriations for Fiscal Year 1978*, Hearings before the House Committee on Armed Services, 95 Cong. 1 sess. (GPO, 1977), pt. 5, p. 1177.

8. Office of the Assistant Secretary of Defense (Manpower, Reserve Affairs and Logistics), *Manpower Requirements Report for FY 1980* (Department of Defense, February 1979), pp. IX-16, IX-17.

9. Test score data for the reserve components during the late 1970s are considered unreliable. The tests given during that period were scored incorrectly. An erroneous formulation used to convert raw scores into percentile scores for a new version of the test introduced in 1976 caused the recorded scores to be overstated until the error was detected in 1980. Although the same problem affected regular Army recruits, their scores were later "renormed." The size of the problem was substantial: for example, in contrast to the belief that only 9 percent of the recruits who entered the active Army in fiscal 1979 had scored in category IV, corrected scores placed 46 percent in that category (as shown in figure 5-3). Because raw scores for reserve recruits were not recorded during the period, renorming could not be done. Nonetheless, one can reasonably speculate that the aptitude scores of reserve recruits were probably overstated, on average, to at least the same degree as active recruits.

10. For example, the proportion of Army recruits with below-average scores on the standardized entry test rose markedly: from 17 percent between 1974 and 1976 to 44 percent between 1977 and 1980. See Martin Binkin, *America's Volunteer Military: Progress and Prospects* (Brookings, 1984), p. 9.

problems, however, were somewhat different from those of the parent service. Whereas the latter were explained by changes in the ratio of military to civilian pay, in youth unemployment, and in the value of educational benefits, the links between economic incentives and reserve recruitment were less clear. The Army's reserve components suffered also at the hands of the active Army. According to one account, the "application of management attention, targeted financial incentives, recruiting resources, and command emphasis to reserve problems lagged by several years behind similar application to active force problems."[11]

In 1980, alarmed by the deterioration of overall military manpower, Congress enacted legislation for the active forces that limited to 25 percent the proportion of new recruits who scored in the lowest permissible AFQT category (category IV) and to 35 percent the proportion of new Army recruits who had not completed high school.[12] Although these restrictions did not apply to the reserves, the sizable increases in pay and benefits enacted by Congress the same year spurred the recruitment of bright and better-educated youth in both the active and reserve components. An 11.7 percent across-the-board increase in military basic pay and allowances in 1980, combined with a 14.3 percent increase in 1981, raised the pay of members of the armed forces nearly a third in just two years.[13]

These pay raises came at a time of recession and further deterioration in the civilian job prospects of American youth; the unemployment rate among 16- to 19-year-old males reached 20.1 percent by 1981. Recruiting for the Army reserves was aided also by new enlistment bonuses and educational tuition grants. Recruitment responsibility for the Army Reserve, meanwhile, was shifted to the better-equipped active Army Recruiting Command, which intensified reserve recruiting efforts by expanding advertising programs and adding recruiters.

Although the separate influences of these factors cannot be measured

11. John R. Brinkerhoff and David W. Grissmer, "The Reserve Forces in an All-Volunteer Environment," in William Bowman, Roger Little, and G. Thomas Sicilia, *The All-Volunteer Force after a Decade: Retrospect and Prospect* (Pergamon-Brassey's, 1986), p. 211.

12. Department of Defense Authorization Act, 1981, P.L. 96-342, sec. 302, 94 Stat. 1077, 1082 (1980).

13. Office of the Assistant Secretary of Defense (Manpower, Reserve Affairs and Logistics), *Manpower Requirements Report for FY 1984* (Department of Defense, 1983), p. IX-4. The 1980 rise was accompanied by a substantial increase in the number and size of bonuses; the overall increase in average military compensation in 1980 amounted to roughly 17 percent.

with precision, the Army's reserve components expanded substantially during the early 1980s, and the qualitative characteristics of new recruits improved as well, especially in the Army Reserve. Between fiscal 1981 and 1987 the Army National Guard grew by about 63,000 and the Army Reserve by roughly 82,000 (figure 5-1). New Army Reserve recruits counted as high school graduates grew from 61 to 96 percent between 1981 and 1987, and their share in the Army National Guard increased from 68 percent in 1981 to 87 percent by 1986 before dropping slightly in 1987 (figure 5-2). The proportion of Army Reserve recruits with below-average aptitude plummeted, from 30 percent in 1981 to 5 percent in 1987. The results for the Army National Guard were somewhat less dramatic; the proportion of Guard recruits with scores below the 31st percentile fell between 1981 and 1983 before again beginning to rise; by 1987 the proportion had returned to the 1981 level (figure 5-3).

Army reservists today, it should be mentioned, bear little resemblance to their much-maligned draft-era predecessors. Compared with the typical person who entered the Army Reserve in 1971, the average recruit in the late 1980s is not as well educated, and does not score as high on the standardized entry test (table 5-1) but, being a true volunteer, is better motivated. The force has also undergone a social transformation, from a virtual white-male bastion in 1971 to an organization that, like the active Army, represents the broader spectrum of American society.

Growth in Full-Time Cadre

In recent years the reserves have also benefited from more full-time personnel to train, supply, maintain, administer, and manage the force. The number of full-time personnel in the Army National Guard, for example, increased from just over 29,000, or 8 percent, in fiscal 1980, to more than 54,000, or almost 12 percent, in fiscal 1987. Similarly, full-time personnel in the Army Reserve grew from about 17,000 in fiscal 1980 to 25,600 in fiscal 1987. By fiscal 1989, according to recent projections of Selected Reserve strength, full-time personnel will account for about 12 percent of the Guard component and approach 9 percent of the Army Reserve component.[14]

14. Fiscal 1980 figures from Reserve Forces Policy Board, *Fiscal Year 1983 Readiness Assessment of the Reserve Components* (Department of Defense, Office of the Secretary of Defense, 1984), pp. 142, 145. Fiscal 1987 data and fiscal 1989 projections from Office of the Assistant Secretary of Defense (Force Management and Personnel) and others,

Table 5-1. Comparison of Characteristics of Army Reserve Recruits (Selected Reserve), Fiscal Years 1971 and 1987

Percent

Characteristic	1971	1987
Educational level[a]		
Some college	63.9	3.7
High school graduate[b]	32.1	92.2
Non-high school graduate	4.0	4.1
AFQT category[a]		
I	18.2	6.0
II	42.1	37.5
III	33.7	51.3
IV	6.1	5.2
Gender		
Male	99.3	72.3
Female	0.7	27.7
Race		
White	99.1	67.9
Nonwhite[c]	0.9	32.1

Sources: Fiscal 1971 data adapted from *Military Posture and Department of Defense Authorization for Appropriations for Fiscal Year 1978*, Hearings before the House Committee on Armed Services, 95 Cong. 1 sess. (Government Printing Office, 1977), pt. 5, pp. 1181, 1183, 1188, 1189; fiscal 1987 data adapted from Assistant Secretary of Defense (Reserve Affairs), *Official Guard and Reserve Manpower Strengths and Statistics, FY 1987 Summary* (Department of Defense, 1987), pp. 233, 248. Figures are rounded.

a. Fiscal 1971 data include males only.

b. Includes high school seniors and those with high school equivalency.

c. Fiscal 1971 data include blacks only.

Especially conspicuous are the huge increases in the numbers of reservists in the Active Guard/Reserve category. Over fiscal 1980–87 AGR personnel grew from 3,218 to 25,237 in the Army National Guard and from 3,999 to 12,414 in the Army Reserve.[15] This trend has become a bone of contention, largely because of the relatively high cost of personnel in this category. The Congressional Budget Office has estimated, for example, that whereas the pay and benefits of the average person on active duty was $29,100 in fiscal 1986, the average pay rate for AGR personnel was about $42,000, with the difference attributed to the higher average entry pay grade for AGR personnel joining the reserves.[16]

The Senate Armed Services Committee has been largely responsible for holding the growth in AGR personnel well below the Reagan admin-

---

Manpower Requirements Report for FY 1989 (Department of Defense, March 1988), pp. III-45, III-58.

15. Ibid.

16. Congressional Budget Office, *Improving the Army Reserves* (November 1985), p. 35.

istration's earlier projections. It denied the administration's entire requested increase for fiscal 1986 and later, in considering the fiscal 1987 budget, made its concerns explicit:

> The committee is concerned that the compensation and benefit program available to full-time reserve and guard members is virtually identical to that available to active duty personnel, despite the different conditions of service between these two groups. In addition, the committee believes that providing full-time support . . . by rotating Active Component personnel into National Guard and reserve units would improve the cohesion and the cooperation between the Active and Reserve components.

The committee further warned the administration of its intention, when reviewing the fiscal 1988 request, "to seriously consider reducing the current number [of AGR personnel] . . . and replacing these individuals with personnel from the Active Components."[17]

The Army, for its part, has resisted efforts to increase the number of regular soldiers on duty with reserve units, especially without an accompanying increase in its end-strength. The Army has also noted that "active-duty soldiers experience considerable difficulties when assigned to Reserve Component units out of the mainstream of the Army establishment." Active-duty soldiers avoid reserve duty because, for one thing, active units are better equipped than reserve units, and for another, they are perceived to have more important missions.[18]

Nonetheless, having available a core group of full-time personnel working on a day-to-day basis unquestionably makes operations on weekends and during annual training more efficient. The high state of readiness of the Air National Guard can be attributed in large measure to the high proportion of full-time members (close to 30 percent in fiscal 1986) on its rolls.[19] Of course, as the ratio of full-time to part-time reservists increases so does the ratio of reserve to active costs. Moreover, since the link between full-time manning and unit readiness has not been precisely defined, the point of diminishing returns has not been estab-

17. For a discussion of the committee's action on the fiscal 1986 request, see *National Defense Authorization Act for Fiscal Year 1986*, S. Rept. 99-41, 99 Cong. 1 sess. (GPO, 1985), p. 186. For 1987, see *National Defense Authorization Act for Fiscal Year 1987*, S. Rept. 99-331, 99 Cong. 2 sess. (GPO, 1986), p. 212; for fiscal 1988, see p. 213.

18. Larry Carney, "Army Wants Lid on Active-Duty Reserve Billets," *Army Times*, May 11, 1987, p. 19.

19. *Reserve Component Programs, Fiscal Year 1987: Annual Report of the Reserve Forces Policy Board*, pp. 24, 53.

Figure 5-4. **Size of the Army Individual Ready Reserve, Fiscal Years 1964–90[a]**

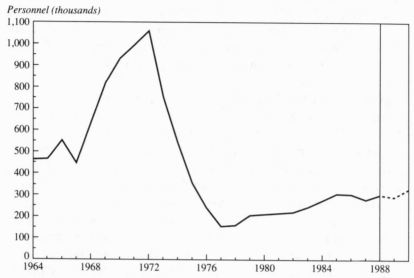

Personnel (thousands)

Sources: Data for fiscal 1964–77 from *America's Volunteers*, p. 221; fiscal 1978–86 data from Major General William F. Ward, chief, Army Reserve, *The Posture of the Army Reserve—FY88* (U.S. Army Reserve), p. 37; and fiscal 1987 figure and fiscal 1988–90 projections from *Manpower Requirements Report for FY 1989*, p. III-59.
  a. Trend for 1988–90 is projected.

lished and the goal for the Army reserves—15 percent full-time manning by 1990—has been open to question.[20]

IRR Trends

Manning of the Individual Ready Reserve (IRR) has also been a source of concern. As indicated in chapter 2, the end of conscription and of the Vietnam War drastically reduced the IRR pool, diminishing it by an order of magnitude between 1972 and 1977. Later efforts to replenish this source of trained military manpower have had only modest success so far; additional gains are expected by the early 1990s, but even then the projected numbers will fall short of the mobilization requirements envisioned by the Army.

During the Vietnam War the Army's IRR grew rapidly (figure 5-4) as the size of the Army and the number of two-year draftees both swelled. At that time, everyone serving in the Army incurred a six-year obligation,

20. Congressional Budget Office, *Improving the Army Reserves*, p. 36 and especially note 3.

and many sought to complete it in the IRR, a less-intrusive option than the Selected Reserve.[21] By fiscal 1972 the IRR pool topped one million before starting to recede as Army strength was cut, draft calls were eliminated, volunteers signed up for longer active-duty tours, and the Army placed greater emphasis on keeping the ranks of its Selected Reserve units filled.

By the end of the Ford administration, officials were paying more attention to the shrinking IRR. In his final posture statement, Secretary of Defense Donald H. Rumsfeld identified the possibilities for reversing the downward trend: extend the length of the military obligation for active and reserve volunteers and eliminate the provision permitting reservists, simply by request, to transfer from the IRR to the Standby Reserve for their last year of obligated service.[22]

The strength of the Army's IRR, nonetheless, continued to plunge, dropping below 200,000 in fiscal 1977. Officials in the Carter administration, however, were cautious in expressing concern. Instead, they focused on analyzing the Army's stated requirement for trained people in the IRR and jousted with that service over the size of the shortfall. The assistant secretary of defense for manpower, reserve affairs and logistics during that period later wrote: "Determining a requirement for the Army IRR has been a very difficult process for the Defense Department. Statements of the requirement have fluctuated between 400,000 and 750,000, and the shortfall has been held to be anything from zero to 350,000."[23]

Differences of opinion turned on assumptions about the "show rate," the casualty rate, and the units needing IRR fillers. The Army's need for a 750,000-man IRR was based on the assumption that 70 percent would show up, meaning that for every 100 trained individuals needed, 143 would have to be called up. But other Defense officials argued "that it would make more sense to take whatever action is required to achieve a

21. There was a complex patchwork of active and reserve options for fulfilling a six-year military service obligation, including (1) three years active duty, two years Individual Ready Reserve, one year Standby Reserve; (2) two years active duty, two years Selected Reserve, two years Standby Reserve; or (3) six months active duty and the remainder in the Selected Reserve.

22. *Department of Defense Annual Report to the Congress, Fiscal Year 1977*, p. 295.

23. Robert B. Pirie, Jr., "The All-Volunteer Force Today: Mobilization Manpower," in Andrew J. Goodpaster, Lloyd H. Elliott, and J. Allan Hovey, Jr., eds., *Toward a Consensus on Military Service: Report of the Atlantic Council's Working Group on Military Service* (Pergamon Press, 1982), p. 126.

yield of 90-95 percent," thus reducing the requirement by as many as 200,000 people.[24] These officials also questioned the projected casualty rates being used by Army planners, which indicated a need by M + 90 for 392,000 casualty replacements in fiscal 1987, much larger than the estimate of 225,000 made for fiscal 1982. Finally, skeptics raised questions about the need to earmark manpower for "phantom" units for which equipment had not been set aside.[25]

A compromise between the Army and the Office of the Secretary of Defense was finally struck in 1979, pegging the IRR requirement at about 480,000, thus acknowledging a shortfall of roughly 270,000.[26] Congress, meanwhile, passed legislation in 1978 directing the Army (but not the other services) to retain IRR personnel who were deemed ineligible for reenlistment in the active Army for administrative reasons but who were eligible to receive an "honorable discharge" or a discharge "under honorable conditions."[27] This change swelled the ranks of the Army's IRR, and by 1987 the new group—called the TLDP, for "Transfer in Lieu of Discharge Program"—was about 44 percent of the Total Army IRR.[28] The Carter administration also initiated a group of measures designed to build up the IRR,[29] which was expected to reach 400,000 by fiscal 1985.[30] As figure 5-4 shows, this schedule was far too optimistic, and by the latest projections available, the Army will have barely 328,100 in its IRR by the end of the decade.

While the size of the shortage continues to be debated, the Army estimated in 1987 that the IRR was not large enough to meet the needs for pretrained manpower in the first ninety days after mobilization, falling 45,000 short under standard mobilization calculations.[31] Even this prediction may be too optimistic, since recent evidence suggests that

24. Ibid.
25. Ibid., p. 127. For a discussion of the casualty replacement issue, see Reserve Forces Policy Board, *Fiscal Year 1981 Readiness Assessment of the Reserve Components* (Department of Defense, Office of the Secretary of Defense, 1981), pp. 31–37.
26. Pirie, "All-Volunteer Force Today," p. 127.
27. *Department of Defense Appropriation Authorization Act, 1979*, H. Rept. 95-1118, 95 Cong. 2 sess. (GPO, 1978), p. 106.
28. Data provided by Office of the Assistant Secretary of Defense (Reserve Affairs), May 1988.
29. For a complete list of these initiatives, see *Department of Defense Annual Report to the Congress, Fiscal Year 1980*, pp. 287–88.
30. Pirie, "All-Volunteer Force Today," p. 128.
31. *Reserve Component Programs, Fiscal Year 1987: Annual Report of the Reserve Forces Policy Board*, p. 44. This calculation assumed show rates of 90 percent for officers and 70 percent for enlisted reservists.

the show rate would probably be smaller than the 70 percent figure usually assumed for enlisted reservists.[32] In a test conducted in fiscal 1987, in which 197,000 members of the IRR were ordered to muster for one day to determine how many reservists could be reached and how many would show up, 104,000 (53 percent) actually reported. The screening of about 11,000 members was cancelled because of lack of funds; assuming that all of these reservists would have reported, the show rate would still have been only about 56 percent.[33]

The situation should improve in the early 1990s when the first effects are felt of legislation enacted in 1983 extending the military service obligation from six to eight years.[34] Although over time this measure will enlarge the IRR pool substantially, some planners wonder about the perishability of military skills, since members of the IRR do not train regularly. "Without retraining," the Reserve Forces Policy Board has contended, "the value of the additional two years . . . is somewhat suspect."[35]

Training

More and better-educated recruits do not alone guarantee greater military capability. Reservists need to acquire and then maintain particular skills and, where circumstances require cohesion and teamwork, they need to train collectively.

To acquire the requisite skills, new recruits for the Army's reserve components first undergo initial training at an active Army training center. Eight weeks are devoted to "basic" training, during which the new soldier is introduced to military life and given intensive physical conditioning and instruction in basic combat skills, including the use of weapons. Following this indoctrination, the enlistee attends "initial skill training," a course in which he or she learns the skills for a specific

32. Ibid.
33. Ibid., pp. 45–46; and data provided by Office of the Assistant Secretary of Defense (Reserve Affairs), May 1988. Among those members who had entered the IRR under the provisions of the TLDP, it should be noted, only 33 percent showed up.
34. P.L. 98-94, sec. 1022, 97 Stat. 614, 670 (1983); and Department of Defense, "Fulfilling the Military Service Obligation," DOD Directive 1304.25 (March 17, 1986).
35. Reserve Forces Policy Board, *Fiscal Year 1984 Readiness Assessment of the Reserve Components* (Department of Defense, Office of the Secretary of Defense, 1985), p. 50.

military job at the apprentice level. Course lengths vary with the complexity of the subject; the average for close to 500 initial skill training courses offered by the Army is fifty-five academic days.[36] For certain skills, the Army's One-Station Unit Training (OSUT) program combines recruit and initial skill training into one course at a single location, thus saving about four weeks in the training cycle.

Because most reservists have civilian employment or school commitments, the reserve unit must be flexible in scheduling individual training activity. New recruits, for example, can be on a unit's rolls for some time before undergoing basic training and, depending on course availability, some reservists may not complete initial entry training within two years.[37]

Nor is previous training always transferable. Soldiers leaving active service who enlist in a reserve unit, and those who transfer from one reserve organization to another, often do not have skills that match the job requirements of the unit. These soldiers must be retrained, either on the job or in a course.[38] A typical unit thus will have on its roster, both at the recruit and prior-service levels, soldiers who are not qualified for their job assignments.[39]

Obviously, the more untrained reservists in a unit, the harder it is to train collectively and hence reach the desired "readiness" status.[40] As

---

36. Office of the Assistant Secretary of Defense (Force Management and Personnel) and others, *Military Manpower Training Report for FY 1987*, vol. 4: *Force Readiness Report* (Department of Defense, March 1986), pp. v-5, v-7.

37. Since 1978 the Army has given reservists a split-training option, under which an individual can take basic training one summer and advanced individual training a year later, receiving drill pay in between. See Crossland and Currie, *Twice the Citizen*, pp. 237–38.

38. The potential for receiving on-the-job training, especially for highly technical skills, is limited for the reserves. Consider the case of the graduate of the Army's course for vehicle mechanics, who would typically require further on-the-job training to reach full proficiency. A soldier in the active Army could be assigned to one of 58 places, each with an average of thirty-five people having the same skill. By contrast, the reservist could be assigned to one of 627 units, each with an average of four people with the same skill. See Michael Ganley, "Who's Guarding the Guard and Reserve?" *Armed Forces Journal International*, May 1986, p. 66.

39. U.S. Army Training Board, *Enhancing Reserve Component Unit Training* (May 1987), p. 14.

40. Under the readiness reporting system, a unit is considered "not ready" in the personnel category if less than 70 percent of its assigned strength is present for duty, if less than 65 percent of its senior enlisted personnel are available, or if less than 65 percent of its assigned personnel are fully trained and "qualified to perform the duties

Figure 5-5. Trends in Skill Training, by Army Reserve Component, Fiscal Years 1975–87

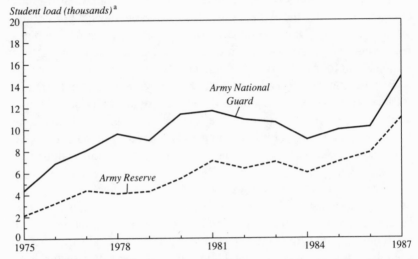

Student load (thousands) [a]

Sources: Data for fiscal 1975–86 and projections for fiscal 1987 adapted from Office of the Assistant Secretary of Defense (Manpower, Reserve Affairs and Logistics), *Military Manpower Training Report for FY 1979* (Department of Defense, March 1978), pp. III-10, v-2; *FY 1985*, pp. III-8, v-2; and *FY 1988*, pp. III-9, v-2.

a. "Student load" is the average number of students attending training courses on a typical workday.

a result, the Army has made efforts to upgrade the training of individual reservists. Substantial growth is evident, for example, in the number of reservists attending skill training courses (figure 5-5) and in their share of classroom seats. Relatively speaking, the proportion of the "student load" allocated to reservists in the Army's skill training courses was projected to more than double, from 12 to 32 percent, between 1975 and 1987.[41] Some expansion in reserve training would have been expected to accompany the growth in the reserves, but the nearly fourfold increase in the average number of classroom seats filled by Army reservists over the period far outran the 24 percent personnel increase.

While individual skills are highly important, tactical ground combat

of the position to which assigned." Army Regulation 220-1, app. D, June 1, 1981, p. D-1.

41. Data adapted from Office of the Assistant Secretary of Defense (Manpower, Reserve Affairs and Logistics), *Military Manpower Training Report for FY 1979*, pp. III-10, v-2; and *FY 1988*, pp. III-9, v-2. The figure for 1987 is based on projected data. Student load is the average number of students attending training courses on a typical workday. It takes into account both the number of people attending training courses and the length of the training program. It is used most often as a workload measure for sizing the training base, but it is also a more reliable gauge than numbers of trainees to assess the training priorities for active and reserve components.

operations are conducted by military units, making combat success greatly dependent on a unit's ability to operate as a cohesive team. Soldiers in an infantry squad, for example, must operate as a team and also must function as an integral part of a platoon, company, battalion, and so on up through the echelons of standard military formations. Above the company level, unit training probably benefits the command and control staff more than the individual soldier.

Team proficiency is arguably less important for noncombat units, in which administrative, logistics, maintenance and other support organizations depend more on individual proficiency than on group interactions. Collective training nonetheless benefits these organizations, too, affording them more realistic operating conditions and the chance to interact with the units they would work with in wartime.

For collective training to be effective, however, the unit's personnel and equipment must be ready. Ideally the unit should be close to full strength, its leadership positions staffed with qualified NCOs and officers, its members able to perform their assigned skills and furnished with sufficient serviceable equipment. Such successful unit training demands a substantial commitment of resources; a stepped-up tempo of operations, for example, consumes more gas and oil, ammunition, and spare parts than normal activities. Also, in the case of combat unit training, facilities large enough to accommodate manuever operations are needed. Finally, enough time must be available for units to attain their readiness objectives.

Because of limitations in personnel, materiel, facilities, and especially time, the readiness objectives of reserve units typically have been less ambitious than those of their active counterparts. Combat readiness at the company level has been the normal—if rarely attained—goal of reserve units, on the assumption that sufficient time between mobilization and deployment would be available to train them up to higher standards, if necessary. As the Army reserves have been assigned more functions that would require their early deployment and preclude lengthy postmobilization training, more attention has been directed toward improving their training readiness.

Of special concern are those reserve combat brigades or battalions that round out active divisions scheduled for early deployment. These units, which will not have the luxury of "shakedown" time after mobilization to integrate their units into the higher echelons of the active structure, strive to achieve a level of combat readiness that minimizes the need for postmobilization training. The problem is less than acute for noncombat units, since as already mentioned they would deploy as detachments, companies, or battalions and thus need less postmobilization training. For example, command and control exercises that promote teamwork among rifle companies in an infantry battalion, among battalions in a division, and so forth, are not as valuable for military police or petroleum supply battalions.

Since the advent of the Total Force policy, officials have instituted several programs designed to improve the training readiness of Army reserve units. One of the earliest, the Affiliation Program, was launched in 1974 to tie high-priority Army reserve units closer to their active Army parent units. Representatives of the active and reserve units interact weekly, and sometimes daily, to plan, coordinate, and carry out training. This closer relationship was intended to enhance the reserve unit's readiness, enabling it to deploy with the parent active unit.

The round-out program has expanded substantially from a relatively conservative beginning in 1974, when only a handful of reserve units were involved. By 1985, as more and more reliance for early-deploying combat strength was placed on the reserves, twenty-nine reserve battalions were used to "flesh out" active Army divisions. Five of the eighteen active Army divisions had at least one reserve combat brigade, and four others relied on one or more reserve battalions to reach their full strength.[42]

For reserve combat units without a round-out affiliation, the Active Component/Reserve Component Partnership Program was established in 1980 to improve the training and deployment readiness of designated reserve forces. Under the program an active unit is designated the partner of a reserve unit based on location, previous relationships, and capabilities. By the mid-1980s, all major reserve combat units were participating in the program.[43]

Defense planners have also given reserve units more opportunities for realistic training through the Overseas Deployment Training Program, under which units scheduled to support overseas contingency plans actually go abroad for some of their training, in many cases with

42. *Department of Defense Annual Report to the Congress, Fiscal Year 1986,* p. 134.

43. Donald B. Skipper, "The Reserve Component Dilemma: Mission vs. Time" (Master's thesis, U.S. Army Command and General Staff College, Ft. Leavenworth, Kan., 1984), pp. 97–98.

the organization with which they will be associated when mobilized. This program, too, has expanded rapidly; compared with only 26 reserve units participating in fiscal 1976, 935 Army Guard units and 1,218 Army Reserve units with more than 47,000 personnel were scheduled for overseas training in fiscal 1987.[44]

Members of the reserve components are also going to more places. In fiscal 1985 and 1986, training was conducted in Europe, the Pacific Basin, Alaska, North Africa, Southwest Asia, Canada, the Mediterranean, and Central America. Deployments to Central America, in fact, became the subject of widespread media attention in 1986, when several governors objected to their state National Guard units taking part in the exercises.[45] These incidents raised an important question about the true availability of national guardsmen. "If the governors can interpose their authority to block training," asked an officer in the Kansas Army National Guard, "could they also interpose state authority at some time in the future to block deployment in a controversial military venture?"[46] In 1986 Congress enacted the Montgomery amendment, limiting the statutory power of a governor of a state to withhold consent "with regard to active duty outside the United States, its territories, and its possessions, because of any objection to the location, purpose, type, or schedule of such active duty."[47]

44. Ibid., p. 99; and *Annual Report of the Reserve Forces Policy Board, Fiscal Year 1986*, p. 71.

45. The initial objections came from the governor of Maine, followed by others, including the governors of Ohio, Vermont, Washington, Massachusetts, California, and Kansas. The governors of Arizona, Mississippi, Nevada, New York, New Mexico, Texas, and Puerto Rico have chosen to consider the question on a case-by-case basis. But the Iowa governor blocked an attempt by the legislature to bar such training and, by one account, twenty-three governors approved of the deployments. See David F. Burrelli, *National Guard Overseas Training Missions: An Issue for U.S. Military Manpower Policy*, Report 86-181 F (Congressional Research Service, December 1986), p. 2; and Samuel J. Newland, "The National Guard: Whose Guard Anyway?" *Parameters*, vol. 18 (June 1988), p. 40. The latter article provides a concise historical account of the controversy that has surrounded the control of the National Guard since the late eighteenth century.

46. Newland, "National Guard," p. 40.

47. *National Defense Authorization Act for Fiscal Year 1987*, H. Rept. 99-1001, 99 Cong. 2 sess. (GPO, 1986), p. 57. The conferees made clear, however, the authority of a governor "to block the training if he or she thinks the guardsmen are needed at home for local emergencies." Ibid., p. 475. In early 1987 Governor Rudy Perpich of Minnesota challenged the constitutionality of this legislation in federal court, based on article I, section 8, paragraph 16, which reserves to the states the authority for training the militia. See "Fight over Guard Control," *Des Moines Register*, July 2, 1987,

In conjunction with the Overseas Deployment Training Program, the reserves are participating in more worldwide training exercises. These joint and Army major command exercises bring together units in a setting that approximates as closely as possible in peacetime the conditions under which they can expect to operate in wartime. Reserve participation in the annual Reforger exercise in Europe has grown in recent years; in 1986, for example, close to 40 percent of the troops deployed from the United States were reservists, including an entire combat brigade of the Army National Guard. Other major exercises in which Army reservists took part in 1986 include Blazing Trails, engineer training exercises in Central America; Bright Star, a combat exercise in the Middle East; and Gallant Eagle, a U.S. Central Command exercise conducted in southern California.[48]

Numerous other unit training initiatives have been instituted in recent years, including the rotation of reserve round-out units through the Army's National Training Center at Fort Irwin, California. With roughly five guard battalions scheduled to accompany their active counterparts each year, this training program—considered the most realistic now available—has been a significant addition.

Finally, much of the credit for recent improvements in the training of the Army's reserves has been attributed to Capstone, a program designed to give reserve units specific wartime missions. Before Capstone, reserve units were required to plan and train for all generic missions; under the

---

p. 10A. The lawsuit was dismissed by a U.S. district court judge on August 3, 1987. Delbert L. Spurlock, Jr., "Reserve Forces: Crucially Important but Unknown," American Bar Association, *Law and National Security Intelligence Report*, vol. 9 (December 1987), p. 2. However, this decision was appealed, and in December 1988 a three-judge panel of the 8th U.S. Circuit Court struck down the Montgomery amendment by a 2–1 vote. "DOD Plans Appeal in Guard Training Case," *Air Force Times*, December 26, 1988, p. 4. In early 1988, Governor Michael S. Dukakis of Massachusetts filed suit to block a two-week training assignment to Honduras and Panama of thirteen members of the Massachusetts Army National Guard, contending that "the Reagan administration is using National Guard training in Central America as part of its ill-advised and illegal strategy to overthrow the Nicaraguan government." On May 6, 1988, U.S. District Court Judge Robert Keeton ruled against Governor Dukakis, upholding the administration's contention that "the 'Army Clause' in the Constitution gives Congress the ultimate say over the nation's entire military apparatus." See "Dukakis Loses Challenge on Sending Troops," *Washington Post*, May 7, 1988, p. A19. Governor Dukakis appealed, but Judge Keeton's decision was upheld by the 1st U.S. Circuit Court of Appeals on October 25, 1988. "Dukakis Loses Appeal on National Guard," *Washington Post*, October 26, 1988, p. A14. Ultimately, this issue will probably have to be decided in the United States Supreme Court.

48. *Annual Report of the Reserve Forces Policy Board, Fiscal Year 1986*, pp. 72–74.

program, which was inaugurated in 1979, the Army "shows the planned wartime alignment of all Active and Reserve Component units, where they are going to fight, in what sequence these units will deploy, and who they will be expected to support."[49]

These initiatives have primarily aided combat units; noncombat activities, particularly combat-service-support units, are given fewer opportunities for unit training. The Army Training Board, for example, found that

> the difficulties of effectively training combat service support units experienced in the [active component] are magnified in the [reserve component] and particularly in the [U.S. Army Reserve] in which most of the CSS [combat service support] units are located. Discussions with trainers at all levels of command about which types of units were the best trained invariably listed them combat arms (CA), combat support (CS), and combat service support (CSS) in that order. CSS units were, by broad agreement, rated the least effectively trained and many senior commanders expressed serious concern over the fact.[50]

This concern is justifiable, according to the board, "in view of the fact that [CSS units] are likely to be the first and perhaps the only [reserve] units required in limited mobilization scenarios."[51] Although acknowledging some technical reasons for the relatively low priority given to the training of CSS units, the board also suggested a possible bias on the part of the Army's training establishment, which is staffed disproportionately by officers with combat arms experience.[52]

The establishment of regional maintenance training sites for maintenance units, consolidated training facilities for military intelligence skills, medical regional training sites, and similar initiatives can be expected to improve the level of CSS training for support units, but more substantial measures will be required if CSS units, especially those slated for immediate deployment, are to meet combat readiness standards.

Equipment

Among the factors that have limited the ability of Army reserve forces to attain desired levels of readiness, equipment shortages have always

49. Skipper, "Reserve Component Dilemma," p. 130.
50. U.S. Army Training Board, *Enhancing Reserve Component Unit Training,* p. 48.
51. Ibid.
52. Ibid., p. 49.

ranked near the top of the list. Moreover, the equipment that reserve units have had on hand has too often been obsolete or in poor condition.

The situation was especially bleak during the Vietnam period, when the flow of equipment to the Army reserves virtually ceased. Equipment that had been ordered for the reserves in the early 1960s as part of Secretary Robert McNamara's program to revitalize conventional forces was diverted to new active Army units as the Vietnam buildup started. Also because of the war the flow of "hand-me-down" equipment from the active Army, which the reserves had traditionally counted on, dried to a trickle. Indeed, in some cases equipment was withdrawn from reserve units for use by active forces. By fiscal 1969, Army reserve components had only a third of the equipment considered the minimum necessary for training, and much of what they did have in inventory was two to three generations behind that of the active force.

The diminished U.S. military involvement in Southeast Asia and attendant reductions in the size of the Army in the early 1970s made it possible for the Army to begin replenishing the equipment stocks of the reserves, a necessary measure if the Total Force initiative was to have credibility. The Pentagon reported that in fiscal 1970, the first year of the resupply program, serviceable equipment worth about $300 million was issued to Army reserve components. Included were M-14 and M-16 rifles to replace World War II–vintage M-1s, M60 tanks to replace outmoded M48 tanks, and UH-1 helicopters.[53] The equipment issued in fiscal 1971, valued at $726 million, included 6,500 tactical radios, about 15,000 wheeled vehicles, 287,000 M-16 rifles, and 52 M60 tanks, with forecasts for $900 million in fiscal 1972 and over $1 billion the following year.[54]

In fact, however, in fiscal 1973 the Army reserves received equipment valued at $682 million, substantially less than expected.[55] This turnaround in the modernization effort was attributed to "the heavy drain placed on Army and Air Force equipment by foreign military sales, epitomized by the resupply of Israel after the destructive Six-Day War in 1973. Hundreds of tanks, trucks, jet fighters, and other items destined for the Guard went to Israel instead."[56] At the end of fiscal 1973, despite

53. *Department of Defense Annual Report to the Congress, Fiscal Year 1972,* pp. 102–03.

54. *Department of Defense Annual Report to the Congress, Fiscal Year 1973,* p. 90.

55. *Department of Defense Annual Report to the Congress, Fiscal Year 1975,* p. 116.

56. W. D. McGlasson, "Combat Readiness Suffers," in Bennie J. Wilson III, ed.,

the large issues of equipment over the previous several years, the value of combat-serviceable equipment in the Army reserve components was placed at $3.66 billion, roughly half of the mobilization requirement.[57]

The reserves' equipment status did not improve appreciably over the next several years. From fiscal 1974 through 1976, the Army Reserve received equipment valued at just over $200 million, bringing it up to about 70 percent of its stated wartime needs.[58] The Army National Guard, meanwhile, reported its fiscal 1976 inventory was valued at $3.5 billion, against a $6 billion mobilization requirement.[59]

Whatever hopes the Army reserves had that the incoming Carter administration would resolve their equipment problems were soon dashed. In 1978 a decision was taken "to increase the Prepositioned Overseas Materiel Configured in Unit Sets (POMCUS), by adding several division sets of equipment to the present two and one-third."[60] Some equipment originally destined for the reserves was diverted to fill POMCUS stocks. Moreover, "the Guard and Reserve not only lost equipment they had expected to receive in the future, but had to dip into their own meager stocks and hand thousands of items back to the Army."[61] The Army Reserve was the most seriously affected; by fiscal 1980 its equipment level fell to about 40 percent of wartime requirements. At the same time the Army National Guard reported being at 70 percent of wartime equipment needs. The major shortages claimed at the time were 2,000 tanks, 10,000 trucks, 5,200 personnel carriers, and 1,150 aircraft.[62]

The Guard and Reserve in the Total Force: The First Decade, 1973–1983 (Washington, D.C.: National Defense University Press, 1985), p. 151.

57. *Department of Defense Annual Report to the Congress, Fiscal Year 1975*, p. 116. But one must exercise caution when interpreting estimates of equipment shortages. The Pentagon's Reserve Forces Policy Board has criticized "the variations and the inability of the Reserve Components or Active Services to accurately or simply display what equipment is on hand, which is first line equipment, what the total authorizations and wartime requirements are in first line equipment, and what second or older generation equipment has been issued 'in lieu of' required line items and is on-hand by Reserve Component units." See Reserve Forces Policy Board, *Fiscal Year 1981 Readiness Assessment of the Reserve Components*, p. 68. The board felt that, on net, these shortcomings led to overstatement of reserve equipment status.

58. Crossland and Currie, *Twice the Citizen*, p. 246.

59. *Fiscal Year 1976 and July–September 1976 Transition Period Authorization for Military Procurement, Research and Development, and Active Duty, Selected Reserve, and Civilian Personnel Strengths*, Hearings before the Senate Committee on Armed Services, 94 Cong. 1 sess. (GPO, 1975), pt. 5: *Manpower*, p. 2575.

60. *Department of Defense Annual Report to the Congress, Fiscal Year 1979*, p. 140.

61. McGlasson, "Combat Readiness Suffers," p. 152.

62. *Annual Report of the Reserve Forces Policy Board, Fiscal Year 1981*, p. 10.

Stock levels aside, reserve proponents were also concerned about the quality of the equipment on hand. Some felt that much of the progress toward modernization under the Total Force policy had been nullified because the equipment being delivered to the reserves was soon outmoded by the rapid pace of advances in military technology. For example, in the early 1980s the Army National Guard was authorized 2,400 helicopters (roughly a third of the total Army fleet), but at least 900 of those it had were considered out-of-date. Some were Vietnam-era gunships, lacking antitank capabilities, and thus considered to be of limited use in a European contingency.[63]

At the close of the Carter administration, the Army Guard was equipped at 69 percent and the Army Reserve at 26 percent of their stated wartime requirements. The costs of fully equipping the Army reserves was placed at $9.1 billion, about $3.7 billion for the Guard and $5.4 billion for the Reserves.[64]

The chances that these funds would become available were heightened in the minds of reserve enthusiasts with the election of Ronald Reagan and his pledge to "rearm America." To be sure, defense spending surged dramatically, and Army procurement programs were among the beneficiaries. The reserves had reason to be encouraged early in the new administration when Secretary of Defense Caspar Weinberger said: "In order to be ready, the Reserve Forces must be furnished with the equipment, manpower, and supplies necessary to conduct effective training. . . . I wish to affirm my belief in—and full support of—the Total Force Policy. The Guard and Reserve are going to be full partners with their active counterparts in this Administration."[65] If the Army got the message, it was not evident in its fiscal 1982 budget or its 1983-88 five-year program. In fact, all of the military services were scored by the Pentagon's Reserve Forces Policy Board:

> The Services maintain that Reserve Component procurement is included within their procurement program but could not, when questioned, identify either an amount or how many of what piece of equipment is allocated for the Guard and Reserve in their plans.
> *The failure of the Services to identify Guard and Reserve procurement*

63. McGlasson, "Combat Readiness Suffers," p. 152.
64. Reserve Forces Policy Board, *Fiscal Year 1981 Readiness Assessment of the Reserve Components*, p. 67.
65. Quoted in *Annual Report of the Reserve Forces Policy Board, Fiscal Year 1981*, p. 1.

gives the impression that equipping the Reserve Components is not a planned process, but rather the Guard and Reserve is equipped with resources left over from equipping the Active Forces.[66]

The Army's failure to demonstrate that it was making an effort to improve the equipment of the reserves got Congress more involved, at the instigation of several of the reserves' strong political patrons.[67] Beginning with the fiscal 1982 budget, Congress appropriated separate funds, over and above those included in the Army's budget, specifically for reserve procurement, as shown below (in millions of dollars):[68]

		Army National Guard	*Army Reserve*
	1982	50	0
	1983	50	15
	1984	100	0
	1985	150	150
	1986	532	365
	1987	146	90
	1988	273	85
Total	1982–88	1,301	705

These funds were used mainly to procure tracked and wheeled vehicles and modern communications equipment. The Army, meanwhile, began giving the reserves some of the latest high-tech weapon systems, including M1 tanks and Bradley fighting vehicles.

The increases in procurement appropriations earmarked for the reserves, however, have been slow to take effect. In 1983, noting the lack of improvement in the readiness of the reserves, the Reserve Forces Policy Board again suggested that the active forces were shortchanging their reserve components: "The Board continues to be concerned with the readiness levels of the Reserve Components. Despite increased defense budgets the Board believes that Service priorities and the modernization programs of the Services have had a negative impact on Reserve Component readiness."[69]

The downward trend in equipment readiness was reversed by 1984.

66. *Annual Report of the Reserve Forces Policy Board, Fiscal Year 1982,* p. 14. Emphasis in original.

67. The Army, however, did institute a policy in 1981 that equipment needed for POMCUS was not to be at the expense of the reserve components. *Annual Report of the Reserve Forces Policy Board, Fiscal Year 1983,* p. 15.

68. *Reserve Component Programs, Fiscal Year 1987: Annual Report of the Reserve Forces Policy Board,* p. 80.

69. *Annual Report of the Reserve Forces Policy Board, Fiscal Year 1982,* p. 8.

Since then the Army National Guard and, to a lesser extent, the Army Reserve have reported improvements. The Army stepped up its deliveries of factory-fresh equipment, and by 1987 four Guard tank battalions were equipped with M1 tanks and four others with updated M60A3s. The Army also announced plans to field the AH-64 Apache attack helicopter with Guard units in fiscal 1988.[70]

Call-Up Authority

Besides the steps taken to enhance the readiness of reserve units, measures have also been taken to improve the chances that their capabilities would be put to use. As detailed earlier, President Johnson's reluctance to mobilize the reserves for Vietnam was due in large part to the international and domestic consequences he believed would follow a national emergency declaration required under then-existing laws. The legacy of that decision is a strong and widespread tendency, especially among Pentagon force planners, to discount the military significance of the reserves, improved though they may be.

In a move designed in part to bolster confidence that future administrations would not avoid mobilizing the reserves, in 1976 Congress granted the president authority to call to active duty up to 50,000 members of the Selected Reserve for a period of not more than ninety days without a declaration of war or national emergency.[71] Both houses of Congress must be notified within twenty-four hours of presidential exercise of this authority.

This legislation gave the chief executive the flexibility to demonstrate American resolve or to begin preparations for mobilization during an international crisis without unduly exacerbating tensions. Supporters

70. *Annual Report of the Reserve Forces Policy Board, Fiscal Year 1986*, p. 52.

71. This legislation was prompted by an Air Force request for some 10,000 extra active-duty personnel and federal civilians to increase their strategic transport capabilities in an emergency. Congress felt that, although more aircrews would indeed be required in an emergency, they would not be needed in peacetime. The mission seemed to Congress to be tailor-made for the Air Force reserve components, to be facilitated by legislation giving the president the authority for "limited selective mobilization of members of the Air National Guard under circumstances not leading to a declaration of a national emergency by the Congress or the President." See *Enabling the President to Authorize the Involuntary Order to Active Duty of Selected Reservists for a Limited Period without a Declaration of War or National Emergency,* S. Rept. 94-562, 94 Cong. 1 sess. (GPO, 1975), p. 4. The law as finally passed, however, was much broader, applying to all Selected Reserves.

also felt that the legislation was needed "to enhance the credibility" of the reserves "in the eyes of our allies, and also as perceived by the active duty and Reserve establishments and the general public."[72]

This legislation could not have been too popular in some quarters of the Pentagon, since the secretary of defense argued in 1983 that "it must be recognized that the U.S. experiences minor demands for surges in certain military activities during peacetime frequently enough that it would be prudent to provide for these occurrences with active forces. . . . Call-up of reservists for these activities may not only send the incorrect political signal, but might occur so frequently that significant disruption of reservists' civilian careers could become a problem for some."[73]

Despite such concerns, the number of reservists that could be called up under this authority was doubled four years later, from 50,000 to 100,000.[74] Two circumstances prompted this expansion. First, "Nifty Nugget," a simulated mobilization conducted in 1978, had shown that more than 50,000 reservists would be needed in the early stages of a mobilization. Second, the newly formed Rapid Deployment Force, established under the Carter Doctrine in the wake of unsettling events in Southwest Asia to respond immediately to international crises, had to rely to a large extent on reserve units.

The number that could be mobilized under this authority was doubled once again, to 200,000, by legislation enacted in 1986.[75] This time the justification, as stated by the House Armed Services Committee, was that "the existing ceiling is inadequate in light of the increased reliance placed on the reserve forces in recent years. A prompt and adequate military response to any conflict other than a very minor operation would be impossible under the existing statutory ceiling, given that one-third of the combat capability and more than half of the combat support capability in the Army are located in the reserve components."[76]

72. Remarks of Senator Sam Nunn, *Congressional Record*, January 26, 1976, p. 982.

73. Office of the Assistant Secretary of Defense (Manpower, Reserve Affairs and Logistics), "The Guard, Reserve and Active Components of the Total Force," Report to the Senate Committee on Appropriations, June 30, 1983, p. 27.

74. P.L. 96-584, 94 Stat. 3377 (1980).

75. P.L. 99-661; text reprinted in *National Defense Authorization Act for Fiscal Year 1987*, H. Rept. 99-1001, 99 Cong. 2 sess. (GPO, 1986), p. 57. This legislation also gave the president authority to extend the period of service to 180 days, if he deems it necessary in the interests of national security.

76. *National Defense Authorization Act for Fiscal Year 1987*, H. Rept. 99-718, 99 Cong. 2 sess. (GPO, 1986), p. 203.

The authority embodied in this legislation, it should be reiterated, applies only to the Selected Reserve, thereby excluding members of the Individual Ready Reserve. By all appearances, this oversight in the initial legislation in 1976 was accidental. Even if the IRR had been considered, however, its exclusion would have been understandable. The limited purposes for which the initial authority was intended could be served without calling on the IRR; there was a widespread lack of confidence at the time that members of the IRR could even be located, much less that they would possess up-to-date skills; and, finally, as suggested in the previous chapter, the recall of individual reservists ahead of units has consistently spelled trouble.

Since recall authority has been substantially expanded, however, and especially since additional early-deployment missions have been assigned to the reserves, the exclusion of the IRR has become more questionable. Should some Selected Reserve units be called up under this authority to support, say, a quick-breaking military operation in Southwest Asia, the Army would have to either fill out the units by cannibalizing other units or deploy the units without their full wartime complements.

CHAPTER SIX

CAPABILITIES AND LIMITATIONS

WITHOUT question, the Army's reserve components of the late 1980s possess military capabilities substantially greater than their Vietnam-era predecessors. Entrusted under the Total Force policy with extraordinary responsibilities for protecting the nation's security, their strength has been increased, their training opportunities expanded, and their equipment shortfalls reduced.

Nonetheless, some observers question whether the reserves could in fact fulfill their new responsibilities. Could Georgia's 48th Infantry Brigade, for example, which rounds out the 24th Infantry Division, move out as early as its rapid deployment mission might require? If so, would it be capable of successfully accomplishing its combat mission? How ready are the many Army Reserve combat-service-support units earmarked for deployment to Europe within a few days of a decision to mobilize? Could they actually provide the logistics support needed to sustain the forces engaged in combat? Would the National Guard divisions slated to reinforce NATO several weeks after mobilization be ready in time?

Current Status

There are no sure answers. Military capability—the ability to achieve a specific wartime objective, such as to destroy a target set—depends on several factors beyond numbers of soldiers, weapons, and other measurable resources; intangibles such as leadership, morale, and cohesiveness must be considered. Assessments of capability are among the most difficult problems facing military analysts.

Table 6-1. Criteria for Readiness Ratings in U.S. Army Reserves under UNITREP System, Mid–1980s[a]

	Condition			
Category	C-1	C-2	C-3	C-4
Personnel (percent)	90	80	70	Less than 70
Equipment-on-hand (percent of items above 90 percent fill-rate)	90	80	65	Less than 65
Equipment condition (percent of high-priority equipment rated mission capable)	90	70	60	Less than 60
Training (weeks required)				
Division, brigade, battalion	0–2	3–4	5–6	Over 7
Company	0–1	2	3–4	Over 5

Source: Congressional Budget Office, *Improving the Army Reserves* (November 1985), p. 17.
a. See text note 1.

A widely used surrogate for capability has been military readiness—the ability of units to deliver the outputs for which they were designed. Readiness is typically measured in five resource categories: personnel strength, individual skill qualification, equipment level, equipment condition, and unit training. Each category is assigned a condition rating, ranging from "fully combat ready" (C-1) to "not combat ready" (C4), depending on the percent of the unit's wartime requirements for people and equipment and the estimated training time required for a unit to reach fully trained status (table 6-1). The unit is also assigned an overall rating, usually the lowest of the category ratings, but subject to adjustment by unit commanders.[1]

Apart from measuring inputs rather than outputs, this system has other shortcomings. Not all units are required to make reports; those that are, do so periodically, thus providing a snapshot in time rather than an average condition. Also, the training-condition rating is largely subjective, depending on the judgment of the unit commander. Despite such limitations, however, the system remains the only means available

1. The Unit Status and Identity Report (UNITREP) system described here and shown in table 6-1 was replaced in 1987 with the Status of Resources and Training System (SORTS), an effort by the Pentagon to downplay the combat readiness connotations of the system. According to the Reserve Forces Policy Board, "UNITREP ratings were erroneously viewed by some as a measure for unit readiness and/or capability when, in fact, the ratings only measured the status of a unit's resources and training." *Reserve Component Programs, Fiscal Year 1987: Annual Report of the Reserve Forces Policy Board,* p. 160. These changes, however, were largely cosmetic: combat condition ratings are now called category levels, equipment readiness is now called equipment condition, and descriptive short titles, such as "fully combat ready," have been omitted. Ibid., p. 160.

Table 6-2. Percentage of Units in Category C-3 or Above, by Army Component, Fiscal Years 1983–87

Component and resource	1983	1984	1985	1986	1987
Army National Guard					
Composite	62	58	60	71	76
Personnel strength	72	75	76	80	83
Individual skill qualification	75	79	78	80	80
Equipment on-hand	56	53	58	79	86
Equipment condition	79	78	79	84	85
Unit training	89	92	91	93	95
Army Reserve					
Composite	41	42	40	45	56
Personnel strength	52	57	53	56	65
Individual skill qualification	53	60	56	60	69
Equipment on-hand	50	50	49	53	71
Equipment condition	76	74	74	77	76
Unit training	84	86	84	86	90

Sources: *Annual Report of the Reserve Forces Policy Board, Fiscal Year 1985*, pp. 5–6; *Fiscal Year 1986*, pp. 111–12; and *Fiscal Year 1987*, pp. 162–64.

for tracing changes in resource availability and for making comparisons between units and components.[2]

If we use readiness as the criterion, both components of the reserve have registered notable improvements in recent years (table 6-2). By this measuring stick, in 1987 the Army National Guard appeared to be especially sound, with 76 percent of its reporting units receiving an overall rating of C-3 or above, up from 58 percent just three years earlier. The improvements are reasonably uniform over all resource areas. Compared with this excellent showing, the Army Reserve, despite its gains, was still experiencing major readiness problems, with only 56 percent of its reporting units in the C-3 or above categories in 1987.

Some are skeptical about the relatively large number of units in both components rated C-3 or better in unit training, given reported deficiencies in resources essential to realistic exercises. The Congressional Budget Office has suggested that these data should be used cautiously, since "some critics believe that the training ratings have an optimistic bias, reflecting the reserve unit commander's 'can do' attitude as much as his unit's readiness."[3]

2. Detailed data generated by the system are classified. Occasionally, aggregated results are published in public documents prepared by the Department of Defense, the General Accounting Office, or the Congressional Budget Office, or are cited in congressional testimony by military and civilian officials.
3. Congressional Budget Office, *Improving the Army Reserves* (November 1985), p. 16.

Two other observations are worth making. First, even allowing for the shortcomings of the reporting system, clearly the Army National Guard is in much better shape than the Army Reserve. On the surface, that finding seems inconsistent with the deployment schedule discussed in chapter 2, which indicated that many Army Reserve support units would be deployed well ahead of National Guard units.

Second, the aggregate figures do not reveal whether most reserve units are clustered near the bottom end of the range (C-3) or near the top (C-1). The difference could be substantial, requiring perhaps five to six weeks' additional postmobilization training for those near the bottom end.

A more realistic picture of the status of Army reserve forces emerges from the findings of various studies and from judgments reflected in congressional testimony and assessments by defense officials. The Congressional Budget Office, for example, found in 1984 that the overall readiness of high-priority Army National Guard round-out battalions was 15 percent lower on average than that of active units. The greatest difference appeared in unit training readiness, where the Guard battalions were rated about 30 percent lower than similar active combat battalions. The CBO also found that, while Army reserve combat units could be expected to meet their designed deployment schedule through M + 60 days, shortfalls of 37 percent in combat units and of 31 percent in combat-service-support units were likely during the first month.[4]

The seriousness of these shortfalls was reinforced in a presentation to the House Armed Services Committee by the General Accounting Office in April 1986: "There are not enough units in the Army's force structure to meet the M + 10 support requirement in some functional areas . . . [and] the capability of existing forward deployed and CONUS-based CS/CSS units to perform their required mission is adversely affected by low levels of readiness. While the readiness of units in the active force is low, the readiness condition of the 70 percent of the support force in the reserves is disproportionately worse."[5]

This view was shared by General Bernard W. Rogers, the former supreme allied commander in Europe, who while still in his post reported to Congress in 1987 that many reserve units intended to reinforce combat forces in Europe "are undermanned, underequipped and unable to

4. Ibid., pp. 20–21, 24.
5. *National Defense Authorization Act for Fiscal Year 1988/1989*, H. Rept. 100-58, 100 Cong. 1 sess. (Government Printing Office, 1987), p. 172.

perform the tasks for which they were formed. As a result," he concluded, "many reinforcing units will be required to remain in [the United States] after mobilization, awaiting essential equipments, additional manpower and necessary training."[6] Also, according to press accounts, after testimony by reserve officials and the GAO before a closed hearing of the Senate Armed Services Committee in 1988, "senators who heard the update on reserve readiness said the message was that these backup forces [the Army guard and reserve] could not support front-line units in a war in Europe."[7]

Among the problems that affected the Army's reserve components in the late 1980s, the scarcity of fully qualified reservists headed the list. In 1986, of a total of 1,772 Army Reserve units (battalion and lower), 643 were rated not combat ready because of low levels of skill qualifications; of these, 228 (more than 35 percent) were slated for deployment in the first thirty days. The picture for the Army National Guard was somewhat better: of 1,656 units (battalion-size and smaller), 202 (12 percent) were rated not combat ready for lack of qualified personnel, 62 of which were earmarked to deploy by M + 30 days.[8]

Even these estimates, however, could be too optimistic, according to the General Accounting Office, which contends that the Army is overstating the qualifications of its reserve personnel. The GAO maintains that the Army counts graduates of advanced initial training courses as qualified in a skill even when a soldier has covered only a fraction of the critical tasks associated with that skill. Reservists who attend Bradley system mechanics training, for example, are taught only half of the critical tasks for that skill, while those in the light-wheel-vehicle mechanics course cover only 29 percent of all the tasks. The remaining tasks, it is expected, will be mastered after the trainee reports to his unit. The result is that "under the best of circumstances, it would take about 1 year, or an additional 38 training days, beyond completion of [advanced initial training] to fully train a reservist."[9]

6. Quoted in Rick Maze, "Growing Reliance on Reserve Raises Concerns," *Army Times,* April 13, 1987, p. 8.

7. George C. Wilson, "U.S. Reserves Called Insufficient for War in Europe," *Washington Post,* April 14, 1988, p. 9.

8. Data obtained from Department of the Army, March 1987.

9. "Skill Qualifications of National Guard and Reserve Members," Statement of Richard A. Davis, senior associate director, National Security and International Affairs Division, General Accounting Office, before the Subcommittee on Military Personnel and Compensation, House Committee on Armed Services, March 10, 1988, p. 11.

Equipment shortfalls also still limit the readiness of the Army reserves, despite the substantial "dedicated" funds appropriated by Congress and the extra equipment provided by the Army to its reserve components through redistribution or new procurement described in the previous chapter. Shortages in tactical wheeled vehicles, communications and electronics gear, and air defense equipment are high on the list. All told, as of September 1986, the Army National Guard reported having on hand only 70 percent of its authorized equipment and placed the cost of meeting these shortages at almost $11 billion. The Army Reserve, meanwhile, reported having 67 percent of its authorized equipment and valued its equipment shortage at more than $2 billion.[10]

Beyond these indicators, little else is publicly available on which to base judgments about the capabilities of the reserves. The views of senior military officials would seem to count, but here too consensus is hard to obtain. For example, one of the most devastating critiques of the reserves has been made by an active-Army general, who concluded in 1986 that "our service is literally choking on our Reserve Components." In a scathing appraisal of the reserves, noteworthy because critical views held by high-ranking Army insiders are rarely aired in public, the official contended that "our Reserve Components are not combat ready, particularly National Guard combat units. Roundout is not working. These forces will not be prepared to go to war in synchronization with their affiliated active duty formations."[11] This judgment clashed with the official position, expressed in 1986 by the Army vice chief of staff, who boasted that the Army National Guard was at its highest readiness level in history and has "demonstrated conclusively to our friends and potential enemies its deployability."[12]

The inconsistency reflected in these views is not uncommon. It is difficult to sort out rhetoric and reality, especially when measures of effectiveness are so inadequate. What can be said with a reasonable

10. *Annual Report of the Reserve Forces Policy Board, Fiscal Year 1986*, p. 35. Both estimates, however, understate the value of shortages measured against wartime important being that Israeli reservists train in longer blocks of time, for example, one amount of equipment on hand may not be a good gauge of a unit's readiness to fulfill its mission; the condition of the equipment and its compatibility with other systems are also key considerations.

11. Letter, Major General Robert E. Wagner, commander, U.S. Army ROTC Cadet Command, to General Carl E. Vuono, commander, U.S. Army Training and Doctrine Command, August 25, 1986, pp. 2, 1.

12. Larry Carney, "Reserve Update 'On Track,' Thurman Says," *Army Times*, October 27, 1986, p. 20.

degree of confidence, however, is that Army reserve units are neither as well equipped nor as well trained as their active counterparts and, as history has shown, a decision to use them carries a great deal of political baggage. The situation would be less worrisome if many reserve units were not being counted on as equivalents of active-duty units, to be deployed early in a war. But, as discussed earlier, many are, and the question left hanging is whether the training, equipage, and political availability of such units can be made consistent with these priority missions and, if so, how.

Those who support the present course are optimistic that these conditions can be met. The full capabilities of the reserves, they contend, will be realized once the programs begun in the late 1970s and early 1980s to improve equipment and training mature. Moreover, they believe that recent legislation liberalizing the president's authority to call up the reserves has depoliticized the mobilization decision.

Skeptics, meanwhile, hold that it is unreasonable to expect reserve units to match the capabilities required of early-deploying forces. For one thing, part-timers cannot train as intensely as full-time soldiers. For another, the reserves are given low priority in internal Army struggles over resources. Moreover, so the argument goes, it is equally unreasonable to assume that future presidents would order a call-up quickly enough for the Army to carry out the deployment sequence specified in its current war plans, notwithstanding an ability to do so without the declaration of a national emergency.

Training Limitations

A principal factor hampering the assignment of selected reserve units to early deployment missions has been their lack of training time. As indicated in chapter 2, under certain contingency plans some reserve units are slated to perform their mission within days of a decision to deploy. Such plans presume, among other things, that the units would be at or near full strength with trained and qualified personnel, and that they would have trained together often enough to ensure the teamwork and coordination required within the unit and, in some cases, between the unit and higher echelon staffs.

Are these assumptions realistic? Not according to a 1984 Department of Defense report:

It is in the area of training that the major capability differences between active and reserve components become apparent. Active units have significantly more training time available each year than do reserve component units (161 days, on the average, as compared to 38–39 days for the reserve components). This greater opportunity to train allows active units to be more effective and to train to the organizational level at which they will be employed, including brigade and division level operations. Reserve component units, however, because of time-to-train constraints, normally train at a lower organizational level, such as platoon and company.

One might assume that given equal amounts of equipment and personnel, active and reserve component units of the same type would have equal combat capability. However, the major differences in available training time between active and reserve component units generally result in a greater initial capability for the active unit. Consequently, these disparate peacetime capabilities to perform wartime missions are reflected in the differences in response times between active and reserve component units.[13]

"Effective" Training Time

The training time advantage of active units becomes more vivid when account is taken of the difference between "available" and "effective" training time for reserve units. By one estimate, a commander of a reserve unit can count on half of the available time (38–39 days a year) at best for productive training. Because of requirements for equipment maintenance, personnel administration, medical requirements (for example, immunizations), and travel time to and from local and annual training areas, "the commander has 15 or fewer days left for training."[14]

Travel time especially affects tactical units, which must train away from population centers. One experienced observer of reserve unit training has described a typical case:

> An Infantry battalion from Buffalo assembles at its armory at 7 p.m. on Friday night, drives to Fort Drum arriving at about 1 a.m. Saturday morning, falls out on its equipment at 8 a.m. Saturday, trains until 11 p.m. Saturday. The unit trains and prepares equipment for turn-in to the equipment concentration site between 8 a.m. and 12 o'clock noon Sunday. . . . [T]he unit must devote 12 out of 31 hours, or 38% of the time traveling. Other units traveling from NYC to Fort Dix . . . spend approximately 44 to 50% of their time traveling.[15]

13. Department of Defense, "Reserve and National Guard Capabilities," Report to the Senate Committee on Armed Services, March 19, 1984, p. 18.

14. Thomas B. Sharratt, "The Reserves: Full Partners at Last, but How Ready?" *Army,* vol. 29 (June 1979), p. 43.

15. Colonel John De W. Pelton, "Reserve Component Combat Readiness in 192 Hours per Year?" (Student essay, U.S. Army War College, Carlisle Barracks, Penn., October 17, 1975), pp. 6–7.

These are not isolated examples. On average, a reserve unit (battalion or separate company) is located more than 100 miles from its headquarters, about 130 miles from its major equipment site, more than 150 miles from its major training area, over 65 miles from a rifle range, and close to 10 miles from a motor pool.[16] By contrast, these facilities for comparable units in the active Army are generally clustered within a several-mile radius.

The inefficient use of available training time, however, has not been confined to combat units having to travel to distant maneuver areas. An Army study in 1975 indicated that only about half of weekend drill time was directed toward mission training, with the remainder accounted for as follows: "Two weekends each year were devoted to preparation for the Annual General Inspection (AGI); two went into recruiting; one was lost to ceremonies and parades; and one was spent in MOS [military occupational specialty] testing." It was estimated, moreover, "that only 8 to 9 days of useful training were being accomplished during the 14-day [annual training] period," because of time "lost to administration" (what the troops call "Mickey Mouse" activities), "weekend passes, parties, PX visits, issue and turn-in of equipment and travel."[17] Despite many improvements since 1975, the situation has not changed markedly. In 1987 the Army Training Board estimated that "on the average an RC unit gets no more than 11 days for effective field training" out of the 14–17 days allocated for annual training.[18]

16. U.S. Army Training Board, *Enhancing Reserve Component Unit Training* (May 1987), pp. 11–12.

17. Cited in Richard B. Crossland and James T. Currie, *Twice the Citizen: A History of the United States Army Reserve, 1908–1983* (Washington, D.C.: Office of the Chief, Army Reserve, 1984), p. 257.

18. U.S. Army Training Board, *Enhancing Reserve Component Unit Training,* p. 10. Comparisons are often drawn between the capabilities of Army reserve units and their highly successful Air Force counterparts. According to a former deputy assistant secretary of defense for reserve affairs, "There is no reason I can see why any type of Guard or Reserve unit which is properly supported and trained cannot match the high state of readiness which has been attained by the Air Reserve Components." See *Fiscal Year 1973 Authorization for Military Procurement, Research and Development, Construction Authorization for the Safeguard ABM, and Active Duty and Selected Reserve Strengths,* Hearings before the Senate Committee on Armed Services, 92 Cong. 2 sess. (GPO, 1972), pt. 3, p. 1686.

However, basing expectations for the Army Reserve components on the successes achieved by the Air Force Guard and Reserve overlooks some important differences between the services. Although the Air Force units' need to operate and maintain sophisticated equipment would appear to be demanding, paradoxically Air Force reserve

Active-duty soldiers, it should be said, do not train every available day nor should it be assumed that every training day is effective. But on the conservative assumption that reserve training time is fully effective and active-duty training time is, say, 75 percent effective, the active unit still trains almost three times as much as a reserve unit.[19] Moreover, when not training, reserves are dispersed in the civilian community, while active force personnel continue living and working together, performing other missions, presumably building cohesion, and using the chain of command. These comparisons render even stronger the doubts expressed by the chairman of an Army Science Board panel on logistics and airland battle: "Can these men and women, who are trying very hard to do a good job, really be adequately trained to do the kind of sophisticated job in two weeks in the summer and one weekend a month when we can barely keep the active component trained on some of these jobs? Our answer to that question is a simple no."[20]

Additional Training Time: Pros and Cons

The need for more training time was identified in a report prepared in 1979 by the Pentagon, which concluded that "high readiness ratings

---

units have found it easier than, say, infantry units have to maintain their proficiency. More Air Force reserve units are collocated with active units; the logistics, maintenance, and administration support is an obvious advantage. The mobility of Air Force flying units allows them to use distant training facilities, so more realistic combat training can be carried out on weekend drills. The nature of the Air Force missions permits a greater concentration on individual training and proficiency, as opposed to the larger maneuver exercises necessary to simulate land combat activity.

Comparisons are also drawn between the reserve forces of the United States and other nations, most frequently Israel. Israeli enlisted reservists, who train for about the same number of days each year as their American counterparts, are considered by most observers to be far more effective. There are many reasons for this, one of the more important being that Israeli reservists train in longer blocks of time, for example, one of 31 consecutive days and three 3-day periods. See John T. Fishel, "Effective Use of the Reserve Components," *Military Review*, vol. 27 (May 1977), p. 61. This more concentrated training program allows time for conducting full live-fire exercises and probably reduces the Mickey Mouse factor. Of course, this schedule is more feasible in Israel than it would be in the United States, where employers are less likely to tolerate such long absences.

19. In fiscal 1987, the average active Army battalion was projected to train approximately 150 days. See Office of the Assistant Secretary of Defense (Force Management and Personnel) and others, "Readiness Implications of Collective Unit Training for FY 1987," p. I-1, in *Military Manpower Training Report for FY 1987*, vol. 4: *Force Readiness Report* (Department of Defense, March 1986).

20. Peter Weddle, quoted in Vernon A. Guidry, Jr., "Training the Reserves," *Military Logistics Forum*, vol. 3 (March 1987), pp. 53–54.

have been achieved by units in which personnel are authorized more than 48 training assemblies per year. Authorization of additional training assemblies (ATA) would reduce or eliminate post-mobilization training and thus permit employment of mobilized Reserve Forces in the early, critical days of a major war.''[21]

In 1982 the Army announced a program designed to provide more premobilization training time to reserve units:

> The fiscal year 1983 budget begins improvements to accelerate and enhance the readiness of Reserve Component units in the D to D + 60 force package by providing full-time training NCO's down to company level; increased funding for selected units for three weeks (21 days) Annual Training; additional JCS exercise participations; an additional 10–15 days of training for staffs to conduct command post exercises with CAPSTONE associates; and an additional 15 days of counterpart training for key personnel.[22]

Additional training time for certain reservists is not a new concept; since the 1960s reserve aviators have been authorized additional flight training periods to accomplish the demanding requirements for maintaining flying proficiency.[23] Other extra training periods have also been authorized to meet specific requirements. Additional training assemblies, for example, provide extra time for command supervision, leadership training for civil disturbances, and special functions, such as nuclear weapons and airborne training. Round-out battalions scheduled to attend the National Training Center have been receiving additional unit training assemblies and extra training days, and readiness management assemblies have been authorized to assist the commander and staff to accomplish management, administrative, and support activities in preparing for normal weekend drills.[24] In some cases the annual training period also has been extended. Units at the National Training Center and those undergoing training for the M1 Abrams tank or M2/M3 Bradley fighting vehicle are authorized three-week annual training periods.[25] The result, according to the chief of the National Guard Bureau, is that the

21. Quoted in Donald B. Skipper, "The Reserve Component Dilemma: Mission vs. Time" (Master's thesis, U.S. Army Command and General Staff College, Ft. Leavenworth, Kan., 1984), p. 52.

22. *Department of Defense Appropriations for 1983*, Hearings before the House Committee on Appropriations, 97 Cong. 2 sess. (GPO, 1982), pt. 3, p. 177.

23. Skipper, "Reserve Component Dilemma," p. 151.

24. Ibid., pp. B-7, B-8.

25. Key personnel often donate weekends and evenings to unit training and management.

average Army National Guard enlisted soldier actually trains forty-seven days a year and the average officer, eighty days.[26] The average Army Reserve officer, it has been estimated, trains seventy-one days a year.[27]

While the expansion of extra peacetime training has undoubtedly improved the status of many reserve units, it has also demonstrated that the point of diminishing returns may be at hand. Experience shows that increasing the number of paid drills and the length of summer training takes a toll on the morale and motivation of many reservists. Reserve recruitment campaigns stress the part-time nature of reserve service, and "the majority of those who join expect to devote one weekend a month and an additional two full weeks a year to military service."[28] The imposition of extra training time often means that reservists, who are already sacrificing some weekends and perhaps summer vacations, will have to sacrifice still more free time or take more time off from their civilian jobs.

Either prospect is unappealing, since both have been identified as primary reasons that people quit the reserves: of 181,000 soldiers who left the Army reserves in 1983, 61,000 cited "employer problems" and another 60,000 indicated "spousal difficulty."[29] In a comprehensive study of the adequacy of premobilization training time, it was reported that "all of the personnel interviewed . . . expressed the conviction that any across-the-board increase in training time *minimum* requirements would result in a mass exodus of Reserve Component personnel due to increased employer and family support problems."[30] The Pentagon's Reserve Forces Policy Board also reported encountering some difficulties with the prospect of three-week training periods. Citing employer problems that require the reservist to use vacation or leave time for any training beyond fifteen days, the board concluded in its fiscal 1986 report that "no attempt should be made to impose extended training period requirements for all elements of the reserve components."[31]

26. "Statement by Lieutenant General Herbert R. Temple, Jr., Chief, National Guard Bureau, before the Subcommittee on Manpower and Personnel of the Senate Committee on Armed Services," 100 Cong. 1 sess., March 3, 1987, p. 7. Presumably some of this additional time is donated, especially by key NCOs and officers.

27. James Kitfield, "The Total Force at 15," *Military Forum*, vol. 4 (January–February 1988), p. 52.

28. Skipper, "Reserve Component Dilemma," p. 160.

29. Ibid., p. 161.

30. Ibid., p. 163. Emphasis in original.

31. *Annual Report of the Reserve Forces Policy Board, Fiscal Year 1986*, p. 70.

These concerns are justified if the experience of units taking their annual training at the National Training Center is any indication. The NTC experience has generally been viewed as a catalyst for improvements in reserve unit readiness, but it may also be a source of retention problems. Reserve units scheduled for the NTC, desirous of making a good showing, typically undergo prolonged and intensive preparations ("train up" in Army jargon) involving extra training and drills. The preparation of the first National Guard battalion to attend NTC in 1983 and its effects on its members has been described:

> In addition to the required one weekend drill per month, there were additional weekend drills, and longer drills . . . [and] for NCOs and officers, there were also supplemental planning and leadership training during the week for no pay. On top of all this preparatory training, NTC itself requires an extra week of annual training time. . . . [I]t is no wonder that many NCOs and Officers reported not seeing their families on weekends for months at a time.[32]

Besides causing problems at home, NTC training creates problems at work also. A sample of seven units attending the NTC revealed that they suffered attrition rates about 25 percent higher on average than comparable units that did not attend the NTC.[33]

Resetting Training Objectives

Aware of the training limits imposed by such constraints, the Army Training Board in 1987 recognized the futility of attempting to train reserve units up to active standards and took issue with that goal:

32. Glenda Y. Nogami and David W. Grissmer, "Case Studies of Seven Army National Guard Units Attending the National Training Center," in H. Wallace Sinaiko and Kenneth J. Coffey, eds., *Reserve Manpower, Personnel and Training Research* (Smithsonian Institution, Manpower Research and Advisory Services, 1986), p. 56.

33. David W. Grissmer and Glenda Nogami, "Retention Patterns for Army National Guard Units Attending the National Training Center," Personnel Utilization Technical Area Working Paper 87-11 (U.S. Army Research Institute for the Behavioral and Social Sciences, Alexandria, Va., November 1987), pp. 80–81. The authors measured the level of attrition over an eighteen-month period—from one year before to six months after the NTC rotation. In gross terms, the relative attrition rate out of the unit was actually larger—averaging close to 30 percent—but some of these individuals merely transferred to other reserve units.

This is not to imply that reserve participation in NTC should be abandoned. The costs associated with the higher rates of attrition could well be offset by the gains in effectiveness for those units attending the NTC, the premier training facility for the Army. Whether extended drill periods for routine training exercises would be cost-effective is more doubtful.

The Army has placed, with few modifications, the total level of training load expected of AC [active component] units on RC [reserve component] units and has suggested in a variety of ways that they should be able to absorb it. RC commanders have responded to this challenge by attempting to do some of everything and find themselves forced into a position in which the real and implied expectations of the Army are beyond the reach of the time and resources available.[34]

Since the military system places a premium on a "can-do" attitude, reserve units tend to stretch themselves thin and in the process dilute their efforts. "The inevitable result," according to the board, "is that it severely limits the probability of sustaining excellence in any one or group of tasks."[35]

Based on its analysis, the board advocated "doing less, better," since "we cannot recreate the AC training environment for the RC and must, therefore, approach optimizing training readiness in the RC by carefully reducing [by about 50 percent] what is required and supporting execution of those requirements in a variety of ways."[36] This approach seems to deserve further study, especially if the tasks to be reduced are those responsible for most of the ineffective training time today.

Equipment Limitations

Despite the delivery of more equipment to the Army reserves in recent years, up-to-date serviceable equipment reportedly remains in short supply, as discussed earlier. Whether the wartime "requirements" of the Army reserve forces should be the peacetime goal is a legitimate question, especially since they still stand so far short, even after the huge investments in Army procurement in the 1980s.

Addressing the seeming inconsistency of "spending more but getting less," the Reserve Forces Policy Board posed a cogent question: "Why, with all the dollars put into equipment in recent years, hasn't the readiness posture of the Services been raised proportionately?" By their assessment, some of the equipment for which funds have been authorized has not yet been delivered because of the length of the procurement process, manufacturing lead times, or nonavailability. Wartime "requirements"

34. U.S. Army Training Board, *Enhancing Reserve Component Unit Training*, pp. 23–24.
35. Ibid., p. 24.
36. Ibid.

have also been growing with force structure changes and equipment modernization programs.[37]

That explanation aside, the influence of bureaucratic politics on equipment decisions cannot be dismissed. Rivalries between active and reserve components and among reserve components are long-standing. One of the traditional obstacles to developing a credible reserve, according to a former reserve official, was "ingrained attitudes—the 'we versus they' approach—the declination of responsibility for Guard/Reserve problems—the view that any move to upgrade reserves would downgrade Active Forces."[38] While the friction between regulars and reservists seems to have diminished in the Total Force environment, many reservists continue to feel that they have not yet been fully accepted as members of the first team. The attitude was still evident in the late 1970s, as reflected in the views of a commander of a reserve round-out battalion: professional soldiers "of high rank and position" are "throwbacks to the days of World War II and the Korean Conflict . . . [clinging] tenaciously to the shibboleth that Reserve units and personnel are totally incompetent."[39]

By all indications, active-reserve rivalries subsided during the Reagan administration as more resources were made available to the Army. One student of Army bureaucratic politics has said the regulars "are skeptical and concerned, but no longer condescending and contemptuous."[40] But another soldier-scholar wrote that "although publicly the Army leadership is unswerving in supporting what it calls the One Army concept, privately many officers express reservations about the ability of reserves

37. *Annual Report of the Reserve Forces Policy Board, Fiscal Year 1986*, p. 38. Both estimates, however, understate the value of shortages measured against wartime "requirements," which are typically larger than the amount authorized. Also, the amount of equipment on hand may not be a good gauge of a unit's readiness to fulfill its mission. The condition of the equipment and its compatibility with other systems are also key considerations.

38. "Statement of Dr. Theodore C. Marrs, Deputy Assistant Secretary of Defense for Reserve Affairs," in *Fiscal Year 1973 Authorization for Military Procurement, Research and Development, Construction Authorization for the Safeguard ABM, and Active Duty and Selected Reserve Strengths*, Hearings before the Senate Committee on Armed Services, 92 Cong. 2 sess. (GPO, 1972), pt. 3, p. 1625.

39. Harlon C. Herner, "A Battalion Commander Looks at Affiliation," *Military Review*, vol. 58 (October 1978), p. 42.

40. Letter from Lieutenant Colonel Wallace Earl Walker, professor of public policy, Department of Social Sciences, U.S. Military Academy, West Point, New York, January 29, 1988.

to fight on short notice.''[41] This may explain why the Army's investment in the reserves did not grow as much as the reserves had expected. Congress, it will be recalled, had to intervene to ensure that the reserves would receive even modest issues of equipment. Predictably,

> the result is frustration. Early deploying Guard and Reserve logistics units have been told that their role in the Total Army is important. Yet many realize they have neither the equipment nor the training to carry out their missions. . . . The underlying cause of equipment shortages in early deploying logistics units is that the units' missions and deployment schedules have been inadequately considered in Army equipment procurement and distribution plans. Many Guard and Reserve logistics units, scheduled to deploy within 30 days, are assigned priorities so low that only a massive Army equipment procurement program could trickle down enough equipment.[42]

The prospects of such a massive Army procurement program, however, appear increasingly remote. As the Reagan defense buildup lost momentum and faced shrinking budgets for the remainder of the decade, the Army in 1987 announced its intentions to sacrifice equipment buys in order to preserve force structure and sustainability.[43] Reductions or stretchouts in the planned procurement of major weapons, such as M1 tanks, M2/M3 fighting vehicles, and AH-64 Apache helicopters, would delay further the delivery of new equipment or the distribution of hand-me-downs for the reserve forces.

Overall equipment shortages would be less serious if the "first-to-fight, first-to-be-equipped" policy were more rigidly applied. But except for reserve round-out units, it is not. Ideally, continued shortages of equipment should be concentrated among later-deploying units and, indeed, the Army has a formal system designed to ensure that those units who need it first, get it first.[44] While this might be the rule-of-thumb for active Army units, it appears to be less applicable for reserve units. Except for round-out units, which apparently enjoy higher priority, other

41. A. J. Bacevich, "Old Myths, New Myths: Renewing American Military Thought," *Parameters*, vol. 18 (March 1988), note 9 on p. 25.

42. Norman E. Betaque, Jr., "Reservations about the Reserves," *Military Logistics Forum*, vol. 1 (March 1985), p. 42.

43. Tom Donnelly, "Army Plans to Sacrifice Weapons in Wake of Shrinking Budgets," *Defense News*, March 16, 1987, p. 9.

44. The Army designates a priority sequence for allocating resources in peacetime and the early stages of mobilization and deployment through the Department of the Army Master Priority List (DAMPL). See General Accounting Office, *Reserve Components: Alternatives for Equipping the Army's Reserve Components*, GAO/NSID-86-35BR (December 1985), p. 1.

early-deploying reserve units appear not to have been treated any differently than later-deploying units.

A study conducted within the Office of the Secretary of Defense in 1975 found a "lack of effective discrimination between units needed early and those needed late," which was attributed to three factors. First, equipment authorizations tended to be the same for all units. Second, the readiness reporting system was failing to identify problems. And third, too much attention was being paid to later-deploying combat units at the expense of the earlier-deploying, but less glamorous, support units.[45]

Over the next ten years the situation apparently failed to improve; in 1985 the Congressional Budget Office found that the Army Reserve made virtually no distinction between units based on the deployment timetable, although the early-deploying units of the Army National Guard had "somewhat higher authorizations" than did those units scheduled for later deployment.[46] This finding was supported by an analysis of Army equipment-on-hand readiness ratings in 1984, which showed no significant variation among units with different deployment dates, leading the CBO to conclude that "because reserve units are generally equipped at lower levels than active units, this even-handed policy . . . suggests that many of these units expected to provide support early in a war would not have equipment stocks equal to their active counterparts."[47]

In testimony before Congress, the GAO went even further in criticizing the Army's priorities, contending in 1987 that equipment shortages in combat support and combat-service-support units could seriously affect the Army's ability to defend Western Europe. GAO representatives concluded that "although the CS/CSS units identified as being required to support combat forces forward deployed in Europe [the M-day forces] are supposed to have the highest priority for prepositioning material stored in Europe (POMCUS), many of these units have not been authorized for POMCUS storage, and much of the required equipment for those units which [has] been authorized has not been acquired."[48]

45. Department of Defense, *The Guard and Reserve in the Total Force* (September 1975), p. 16.

46. Congressional Budget Office, *Improving the Army Reserves,* p. 21.

47. Ibid., p. 33.

48. *National Defense Authorization Act for Fiscal Year 1988/1989,* H. Rept. 100-58, p. 172.

We have concluded, therefore, that internal Army organizational dynamics continue to present a serious obstacle to the equipment readiness of Army reserve forces, especially combat-service-support units. While the intensity of long-standing intramural rivalries tends to diminish during periods of resource plenty, the competition between the Army's active and reserve components and within its reserve components can be expected to sharpen if, as appears likely, fewer dollars are made available for the national defense. Unless these organizational factors are brought under control, the status of equipment for reserve units is unlikely to improve, nor will its distribution within the reserve components be handled more effectively.

Political Limitations

The wider latitude to call out the reserves that U.S. presidents have enjoyed since 1976 has undoubtedly enhanced the stature of the reserve forces. It has also given the chief executive greater flexibility to meet specific military needs by augmenting active forces, and to generate political signals during international crises. What it has not done, much to the relief of those worried about excessive presidential power, is to remove domestic politics from the equation.

Thus many continue to doubt that the political obstacles to reserve mobilization, such as those that constrained President Johnson throughout the Vietnam War, have been lowered by the expanded authority. "There is the lingering fear," according to one knowledgeable commentator, "that, when needed, reserve forces would not be available because the necessary political decisions to mobilize them would not have been made. . . . The times when you need the reserves most are often very highly charged politically."[49] That opinion was borne out by a survey of senior officers attending the National Defense University in 1982, roughly half of whom "maintained that political and legal restraints would probably delay rapid mobilization of Reserve component units."[50]

These concerns are quite valid. Although an acid test is yet to be

49. Lewis Sorley, quoted in John F. Fitzgerald, "Soldiers Withheld by States," *Hartford Courant,* March 30, 1986, p. A14.

50. James W. Browning II and others, "The US Reserve System: Attitudes, Perceptions, and Realities," in Bennie J. Wilson III, ed., *The Guard and Reserve in the Total Force: The First Decade, 1973–1983* (Washington, D.C.: National Defense University Press, 1985), p. 82.

applied, no president has thus far exercised the new authority, despite many opportunities for doing so. "Between 1976 and 1984," according to one naval analyst, "U.S. Navy and Marine forces alone responded to 41 incidents or crises . . . with an average duration of response in some geographic areas in excess of 100 days. . . . In each case, active naval forces were stretched, deployments were altered and/or extended, exercises were cancelled, leaves were cancelled or delayed, but no reserves were [involuntarily] activated."[51]

The Total Force arrangement was seriously challenged in September 1987, when six naval reserve minesweepers were deployed to the Persian Gulf to support the Kuwaiti oil tanker reflagging operation without most of their reserve crew members.[52] The Navy did not divulge its reasons for leaving the reservists behind, but three possibilities come to mind: it did not consider the reserve crew members competent; it sought to minimize unpopular family and job separations, especially for such an ambiguous and seemingly open-ended operation; or the administration wanted to avoid the escalatory signal that a reserve call-up would convey at a time when it was warding off pressures to comply with the War Powers Act.

The failure to call out the reserves for these incidents is not surprising, given that any mobilization—regardless of whether a national emergency is declared—is a political statement. Presidents must consider not only the escalatory effects in the international community, but also the domestic political reaction, including additional pressures during unfolding crises to invoke the War Powers Act, which presidents have consistently sought to avoid. Thus while the new authority makes it easier for the chief executive to mobilize the reserves, it does not make any easier the decision to do so.

Conclusions

The force of the evidence suggests that the current reliance on the Army's reserve components remains what a former high-ranking Pen-

51. James L. Lacy, *Naval Reserve Forces: The Historical Experience with Involuntary Recalls*, Research Memorandum 86-76 (Alexandria, Va.: Center for Naval Analyses, April 1986), p. 19. Reservists have served on active duty during this period (for example, in Grenada), but these were volunteers.

52. Ted Bush, "Minesweeper Move Jars Reserves," *Navy Times*, September 14, 1987, p. A1.

tagon official called it in 1986, "a serious gamble."[53] Indeed, there is good reason to doubt that units of the Army National Guard and Reserve expected to contribute in the first few days of a military conflict, or even those earmarked to reinforce the active Army several weeks after mobilization, would be able to deploy on schedule without penalties in combat power, effectiveness, and tactical agility. The size of those penalties cannot be predicted with confidence, but the attainment of U.S. military objectives can be tested under various assumptions about the capabilities of the Army National Guard and Reserve.

53. Letter to the editor by James H. Webb, Jr., assistant secretary of defense for reserve affairs, "Why U.S. National Guardsmen Train in Honduras," *New York Times,* October 7, 1986, p. A30.

CHAPTER SEVEN

TESTING THE RESERVES

IN THEORY, U.S. security today depends more than ever before on the Army's National Guard and Reserve. The significance of that dependence for the effectiveness of the Army in combat, however, raises a complex question. Does it mean that the Army no longer can conduct operations overseas without a call-up of some portion of the Guard and Reserve?

The evidence of the past is mixed. As indicated in chapter 4, the Guard and Reserve played large roles in the Second World War and again in Korea. In Vietnam, on the other hand, the U.S. Army committed the equivalent of eight divisions without any major recourse to reserve components; conscription provided the necessary personnel.

Admittedly, times have changed since the war in Southeast Asia. The strength of the regular army has declined, from more than 973,000 men and women in 1964 to roughly 772,000 in 1988, though its force structure is about the same now as it was then. In contrast with 1964, however, combat, combat support, and combat-service-support elements are missing from the current active structure (as detailed in previous chapters). And conscription is no longer available as an easy and cheap way of filling in the empty spaces. Without a draft, even the Individual Ready Reserve has shrunk, so fewer individuals can be called up to fill out understrength units and to replace combat casualties. And while Congress would probably restore conscription in the event of a national emergency, it would take at least four and perhaps as long as six months before inductees could be readied for combat.

Establishing the Strategic Concept

These conditions make the Army's dependence on the reserves look more real than theoretical. And they are reinforced by two other factors.

Whereas in the past the ground forces not deployed overseas were regarded as truly "general purpose"—able to go anywhere, anytime, and cope with any type of enemy—now they are regarded as more specialized to particular regions. Thus a regular Army division or brigade is likely to be committed to or at least earmarked for such major overseas commands as the European Command, Pacific Command, or Central Command, and trained accordingly. Similarly, under the Capstone program, reserve units receive specific assignments to commands and regions. Because of this orientation and the location of bases and active and reserve units, it has become the standard expectation that most regular Army units in the continental United States (CONUS) will be rounded out, augmented, and provided combat service support by reserve components in the event of overseas deployment. Moreover, under current planning, National Guard divisions are seen as being needed almost as quickly as their active-duty counterparts. In fact, nearly twenty years after then-Secretary of Defense Melvin R. Laird first talked about a Total Force, the concept seems to have become a reality.

Despite these developments, it is well to remember that the regular Army, by itself, is a powerful force. Currently, when all separate brigades and armored cavalry regiments in the active forces are counted, the U.S. Army could field the equivalent of eighteen divisions without involving its reserve components. Of that total, ten are garrisoned in the continental United States (along with two Marine Corps divisions). Moreover, despite the growing reliance on the reserves for combat service support, enough of the critical medical, logistic, and maintenance capability remains in the active-duty Army to support eight or nine divisions in combat, although those capabilities are not now deployed to fulfill that purpose. Given the host-nation support to be expected (or agreed to) for U.S. forces in Germany and Korea, this means that, at least in principle, the Army could deploy and sustain a larger capability than it did during the wars in Korea and Southeast Asia. Consequently, the case can be argued that in an era of limited wars the dependence on the reserves during the early stages of a war need not be a matter of great concern. Some might even claim, in the light of the need to respond to such contingencies as Grenada, Nicaragua, and other minor conflicts, that the United States has already overinvested in conventional capabilities and should reallocate resources to "unconventional" forces.

Number of Contingencies

These arguments may very well be right. What they fail to recognize, however, is that the United States for more than twenty-five years has been unwilling to bet on a continuation of the trend to limited and small wars, just as it has been unwilling to bet exclusively on nuclear deterrence as its response to all military challenges. Rightly or wrongly, U.S. conventional force planning has remained focused primarily on what, for lack of a better term, might be called World War III. Only one defense secretary, Caspar W. Weinberger, has come close to referring to such an eventuality when he talked about a worldwide war. His predecessors have preferred to discuss the number of contingencies that might threaten U.S. interests more or less simultaneously and to argue about how many of them, for force planning purposes, the United States should prepare itself to withstand.

The two-and-one-half and one-and-one-half war concepts of the 1960s and 1970s, respectively, consistently understated the complexity of the situations that might arise. And the succession of crises in the 1980s that have occurred in the region of the Persian Gulf, along with revived fears of a Soviet bastion in Central America, as well as in Cuba, have made it clear that the Army, along with the other services, might better plan on the basis of having to deploy to and possibly fight in as many as six different theaters: Norway, Central Europe, Thrace, the Persian Gulf, Korea, and the Caribbean. There have been times, indeed, when Alaska and the Panama Canal have made it onto the list. One way that U.S. and allied forces might be deployed to meet these multiple threats is illustrated in table 7-1.

The prospect of such a worldwide conflagration may seem remote in the late 1980s, especially in the light of the changes that are occurring in the Soviet Union. But it is this prospect that makes the Army's dependence on the reserve components significant and raises the issue of how well the reserve components would respond to such an emergency. Although the Army is not ideally deployed to do so, it has the capability in its active-duty forces of establishing a forward defense, in conjunction with allies, against all but the very largest single assaults that the Soviet Union and its cohorts might undertake. However, even though the Army would probably not be called on to reinforce the northern or southern

Table 7-1. Hypothetical Deployment of U.S. and Allied Ground Forces
Number of division-equivalents

Theater	United States		Allies	Total
	Army	Marine Corps		
North Norway	. . .	1	4	5
Central Europe	23	. . .	39⅔	62⅔
Thrace	. . .	1	3	4
Saudi Arabia	8	1	. . .	9
Korea	2	1	21	24
Caribbean	1⅔	. . .	. . .	1⅔
Iceland	⅓	. . .	. . .	⅓
Alaska	⅓	. . .	. . .	⅓
Panama Canal	⅓	. . .	. . .	⅓
Total	35⅔	4	67⅔	107⅓

Source: Authors' estimates.

Table 7-2. U.S. Ground Force Geographical Deployments, by Component, 1987

Location	Army division-equivalents		Marine Corps divisions	
	Active	Reserve	Active	Reserve
Continental U.S.	10	17	2	1
Europe	5⅔	. . .	. . .	. . .
Korea	1	. . .	. . .	. . .
Okinawa	. . .	. . .	1	. . .
Alaska	⅓	⅓	. . .	. . .
Hawaii	⅔	. . .	. . .	. . .
Puerto Rico	. . .	⅓	. . .	. . .
Panama Canal	⅓	. . .	. . .	. . .
Total	18	17⅔	3	1

Sources: *Department of Defense Annual Report to the Congress, Fiscal Year 1985*, p. 115; *Fiscal Year 1986*, pp. 134–35; *Fiscal Year 1988*, p. 152; and as outlined in chapter 2.

flanks of Europe (Marine Corps responsibilities) and would share responsibility with the marines in the Persian Gulf and Korea as well, it
could not possibly undertake its share of these multiple burdens without
the full use of the 18 division-equivalents in its active-duty structure, the
17⅔ division-equivalents in the reserve components, deployed as shown
in table 7-2, and all the combat-service-support units in both the active
and reserve structure. It should be added that these numbers and four
marine divisions are virtually identical with what the Joint Chiefs of
Staff, five years ago, considered to be the appropriate size of the U.S.
ground forces needed by 1991, although the allocation between active
and reserve units is quite different.

Force Planning Objectives

It is the exception rather than the rule that current force planning calculates the size and composition of the forces needed to fight a major war from start to finish. Since the United States is unlikely to have any grand plan for major military initiatives, not only must it leave to its opponents the choice of where, when, and how to attack; for the most part, it must also leave to a later date decisions about what its ultimate military objectives will be, especially in a world shadowed by nuclear weapons.

Military force planning, therefore, will tend to focus on dealing with the initial stages of a conflict and on containing the enemy as far forward as time and circumstances permit. Accordingly, the Pentagon has set as its goal the rapid mobilization and deployment of enough forces to establish and sustain a forward defense in such key theaters as Central Europe, the Persian Gulf, and South Korea until such time as reinforcements can arrive. During this time not only is the expensive business of trading allied space for time to be avoided; allied leaders will also be expected to mobilize further resources and decide on the longer-term objectives for their forces.

At the present time, however sensible these initial goals, the United States and its allies cannot have high confidence (based on a number of measures) that it will reach all of them, quite apart from the readiness and combat effectiveness of U.S. reserve components. The United States currently lacks the airlift and fast sealift necessary to deal with simultaneous emergencies in Central Europe, the Persian Gulf, and Korea. While the allies with responsibilities for the defense of Central Europe have the force structure necessary for the forward defense of that theater (in conjunction with the United States), their reserve units are short of training and modern equipment. Some efforts have gone forward to prepare defensive positions along the West German frontier, but a great deal more could profitably be done. Neither the United States nor its allies have invested enough in close air support aircraft. And there remains a serious question as to whether they have acquired enough war reserve stocks to permit their forces to outlast the enemy.[1]

In these circumstances, even if the U.S. reserve components were to

1. For a discussion of these shortcomings, see William W. Kaufmann, *A Reasonable Defense* (Brookings, 1986), pp. 75–81.

perform up to the expected standards of their active-duty counterparts, so many other things could go wrong that the effectiveness of the U.S. reserves would not be a decisive factor in whatever failures might occur. The United States thus is in the somewhat peculiar situation that, with its active-duty forces, it can probably handle one fairly large contingency or several small emergencies, but is unable to deal effectively with the worldwide conflict that is the focus of its force planning.

The "Ideal" Force

Suppose, however, that all the deficiencies in current U.S. and allied capabilities were somehow removed and that the augmented ground and close air support forces could deploy in a timely fashion more or less simultaneously to forward positions in Germany, the northern frontier of Saudi Arabia, and the boundary between North and South Korea. Suppose further that all reserve combat units were equal to their active-duty components in combat power and effectiveness, and that they had the necessary logistical systems and war reserve stocks in place to sustain the combat forces without interference from enemy attacks. How well could these ideal forces (as already outlined in table 7-2) be expected to perform, leaving aside such factors as generalship, tactics, terrain, weather, morale, and luck? In short, how well would the planners have calculated U.S. and allied needs relative to the capabilities that their enemies could be expected to muster on standard assumptions about their rates of mobilization and deployment?

The main contingencies and the opposing ground orders of battle are listed in table 7-3. In all three theaters, it is assumed that U.S. and allied forces gain air superiority. Fortified positions are assumed to exist along the frontiers of West Germany and South Korea, but not along the northern border of Saudi Arabia. The main influences on the outcomes of these campaigns, aside from the combat power and effectiveness of the opposing forces, are (a) the ability of the enemy to concentrate a portion of its ground forces at a particular sector of the front, and the ability of friendly forces to counter that concentration; (b) the effects of close air support on the ground battle; and (c) the impact of fortified positions on the effectiveness of the offense and defense.

The outcomes of these force-testing campaigns can be measured in a variety of ways. However, given the force planning objective of being

Table 7-3. Major Contingencies and Opposing Ground Orders of Battle
Number of division-equivalents

Place and time of enemy attacks	U.S.	Allied	Total	Total	Non-Soviet	Soviet
Central Europe						
M+4[a]	5⅔	24⅔	30⅓	30	11[b]	19
M+9	9	34	43	57	31[b]	26
M+14	12	34	46	90	31[b]	59
M+120	23	39⅔	62⅔	110	31[b]	79
Saudi Arabia						
M+90	9	. . .	9	13	. . .	13
Korea						
M+90	3	21	24	40	40[c]	. . .

Sources: International Institute for Strategic Studies, *The Military Balance, 1981–82* (London, 1981), pp. 4–10, 27–37; and authors' estimates.

a. M-day is the day the Warsaw Pact begins to mobilize.

b. Non-Soviet Warsaw Pact.

c. North Korean.

able to sustain a forward defense until reinforcements can arrive, the most appropriate measures are (a) the ability of an enemy to achieve a breakthrough in the attack sector as indicated by an index of relative lethality;[2] (b) the calculated result, which is related to that index and to relative combat losses; and (c) if a breakthrough occurs, the number of days taken to achieve it.

Each of these measures requires some further explanation. An attacking enemy would always have some probability of breaking through the defense, even with inferior forces, whether because of surprise, greater tactical skill, or other factors. On the average, however, the defense would stalemate his attack unless his index of relative lethality were higher than 50 percent. Thus, an enemy index of 50 percent or lower would signify that the defender had, at a minimum, held his position and, under some conditions, might have the resources for an effective counterattack.

Furthermore, even if the attacker had substantial superiority in his index of relative lethality, it would take him some time to achieve the breakthrough. The length of time would depend not only on the relative lethality of the opposing forces, but also on the point at which the defending capabilities broke under the pressure of the attack. Obviously, a breakthrough would occur if the forces defending in the attack sector were annihilated. However, the conventional wisdom has it that they would break before that. There is no widespread agreement as to when

2. For a description of this index, see appendix C and especially note 10.

breakpoints are reached, but one Army manual suggests that it occurs when the defending force loses 40 percent of its capabilities.[3]

The time to this particular point can be measured and gives some indication of whether reinforcements could arrive quickly enough to retrieve the situation. In this connection, however, note that, as far as the United States is concerned, the ideal force deploys all available active and reserve ground forces. Depending, therefore, on the timing of the attacks, a considerable interval might occur before additional units could be mustered, equipped, trained, and deployed. Even if the first attack (in Europe) occurred four days after the Warsaw Pact started to mobilize (M + 4), and other attacks did not begin until M + 90 or later, and even if the United States enacted conscription upon the outbreak of the initial campaign, six months could well elapse before further forces would become available. An enemy breakthrough thus would have to be agonizingly slow to allow for this interval.

Of course, an alert defender who was imperiled could always attempt a retreat to a more defensible line and, in the process, trade space for the time in which to obtain reinforcements. But even if such a strategy were to prove successful, the difficulties with it are legion. Furthermore, if the objective of force planning is a sustained forward defense, and the result is a retreat (however warranted), then something has gone awry with the planning.

Fortunately, in the case of the ideal force, no such choices have to be contemplated. Because the force obtains air superiority over the battlefield, has a major advantage in close air support despite dense enemy organic air defenses, and is over three times more lethal on the ground in Europe and Korea, and twice as effective in Saudi Arabia, it is able to stalemate the attacker in all six contingencies examined (table 7-4). The one fly in this ointment is that the attacker might be able to compensate for his losses more rapidly than the defender and thereby recover the initiative while the defense is in a relatively weakened condition. Whether the Individual Ready Reserve is large enough or could be activated rapidly enough to forestall this possibility is uncertain. It is entirely conceivable, however, that the United States alone would suffer more

3. Department of the Army, *Field Manual: Maneuver Control*, FM 105-5 (December 1973), p. D-19. For an excellent discussion of the complex relation between attrition and performance, see Leonard Wainstein, *The Relationship of Battle Damage to Unit Combat Performance*, IDA Paper P-1903 (Alexandria, Va.: Institute for Defense Analyses, April 1986).

Table 7-4. Outcomes of Multiple Enemy Attacks against the "Ideal" Force

Place and time of enemy attacks	Index of relative lethality[a]	Calculated outcome
Central Europe		
M + 4	.22	Stalemate
M + 9	.36	Stalemate
M + 14	.49	Stalemate
M + 120	.50	Stalemate
Saudi Arabia		
M + 90	.48	Stalemate
Korea		
M + 90	.29	Stalemate

Source: See appendix C for methodology.

a. Index of the attacker's lethality relative to the defender. Stalemate occurs when the index is in favor of the defender (at or below .50). A higher index indicates that the attacker would break through; a lower index that the defender would possess the wherewithal to mount a counterattack.

than 200,000 casualties during the first two months of these three campaigns. The Soviet Union, East Germany, Czechoslovakia, Poland, and North Korea would incur even larger losses, although they might find them easier to replace.

The "Realistic" Force

Since the ideal force does not exist, nor will it, without a major change in the allocation of U.S. and, to a lesser extent, allied defense resources, why should one dwell on its size, composition, and performance? The answer, quite simply, is that the ideal force provides a baseline from which to measure any variations in the performance of one or more of its components: in this case the performance of the reserve ground combat and combat-service-support units that are such a large proportion of the U.S. contribution to the baseline force. In the ideal cases these units were treated as equal in effectiveness to their active-duty U.S. counterparts, whether in actual combat or in delivering essential goods and services to the combat zones. The actuality, however, is that they would be less than equivalent. Their equipment is older, they undergo less intensive training, and they rarely engage in large-scale field exercises.

Such differences raise two questions. First, by how much do these lesser capabilities degrade combat effectiveness? Second, all other things being equal, how does this degradation affect the outcomes of the

Table 7-5. Hypothetical Allocation of U.S. Active-Duty and Reserve Ground Forces to Major Theaters[a]

	Active-duty divisions		Reserve divisions	
Theater	Army	Marine Corps	Army	Marine Corps
Central Europe				
M+4	$5\frac{2}{3}$	...	...	...
M+9	$8\frac{2}{3}$	...	$\frac{1}{3}$	...
M+14	$11\frac{1}{4}$	...	$\frac{2}{3}$	...
M+120	13	...	10	...
Subtotal, Central Europe	13	...	10	...
North Norway	...	1	...	...
Thrace	...	...	...	1
Saudi Arabia	2	1	6	...
Korea	$1\frac{2}{3}$	1	$\frac{1}{3}$	...
Caribbean	...	...	$1\frac{1}{4}$	...
Iceland	$\frac{1}{3}$	...	...	...
Alaska	$\frac{2}{3}$	...	...	...
Panama Canal	$\frac{1}{3}$	...	...	...
Total	18	3	$17\frac{2}{3}$	1

Sources: *Department of Defense Annual Report to the Congress, Fiscal Year 1985*, p. 115; *Fiscal Year 1986*, pp. 134–35; *Fiscal Year 1987*, p. 272; and authors' estimates.

a. This represents only one of many ways to deploy U.S. military assets. Depending on circumstances, it might be desirable to deploy more active-Army forces to the Persian Gulf. That option, of course, would mean that fewer such forces would be available for other theaters.

campaigns summarized in table 7-4? Unfortunately, no confident answers can be given to the first question. While the Army makes numerous statements about the readiness of its active and reserve units, none of these statements says much about the combat effectiveness of these units, and there is no agreed way to measure that effectiveness in advance of actual combat. In making the necessary judgments, however, we can apply reasonable assumptions about how reserve units might be allocated to the three main theaters (Central Europe, Saudi Arabia, and Korea), what combat power and effectiveness reserve units could be expected to yield, and how well the reserve combat-service-support units would perform in supplying and maintaining the combat arms. Once these assumptions are made, they permit the recalculation of the campaigns fought with the ideal or baseline force and a comparison of outcomes to see what differences result from degradations in the performance of reserve ground combat and combat-service-support units.

Although it has no official standing, table 7-5 shows one possible allocation of U.S. Army and Marine Corps ground forces. In only one instance in Central Europe—the M+4 contingency—does the force

Table 7-6. Varying Assumptions about the Combat Power and Effectiveness of U.S. Army Divisions

Condition of division	Combat power[a]	Combat effectiveness[b] (daily)
Case 1		
Active-duty; active-duty tactical support	48,000	.0400
Active-duty; reserve tactical support	48,000	.0300
Reserve; active-duty tactical support	36,000	.0200
Reserve; reserve tactical support	36,000	.0150
Case 2		
Active-duty; active-duty tactical support	48,000	.0400
Active-duty; reserve tactical support	48,000	.0200
Reserve; active-duty tactical support	24,000	.0200
Reserve; reserve tactical support	24,000	.0100
Case 3		
Active-duty; active-duty tactical support	48,000	.0400
Active-duty; reserve tactical support	48,000	.0100
Reserve; active-duty tactical support	24,000	.0200
Reserve; reserve tactical support	24,000	.0025

Source: Authors' estimates. Assumptions described in text.

a. Combat power is the fighting value of the force based primarily on firepower scores.

b. Combat effectiveness is a measure of the ability to inflict damage on the enemy during a given increment of time.

consist entirely of active-duty U.S. combat and combat-service-support units (or the equivalent of the latter in the form of host-nation support). In the three other contingencies in Central Europe ($M+9$, $M+14$, $M+120$), in Saudi Arabia, and in Korea, reserve combat and combat-service-support units are involved to a greater or lesser degree. It should also be noted that table 7-5 does not show the allied contributions that are made in the Central European and Korean campaigns. Since their performance is held constant, the larger their contribution the less impact the degraded U.S. forces have on the outcomes of the campaigns.

Table 7-6 provides three different sets of assumptions about the combat power and effectiveness of the active-duty and reserve forces. Several observations about these assumptions need to be made. Although the U.S. Army maintains six different types of divisions in its inventory—usually characterized as heavy (fourteen) and light (fourteen)—along with a number of nondivisional maneuver brigades and regiments (seventeen heavy and twelve light), the divisions shown in table 7-6 do not make any of these distinctions; they are meant to represent average division-equivalents.

In case 1, the effectiveness of such an average active-duty division is

Table 7-7. Outcomes of Multiple Enemy Attacks When U.S. Army Ground Forces Are Degraded

Place and time of enemy attacks	Case 1			Case 2			Case 3		
	Index of relative lethality[a]	Calculated outcome	Days to break	Index of relative lethality[a]	Calculated outcome	Days to break	Index of relative lethality[a]	Calculated outcome	Days to break
Central Europe									
M+4[b]	.22	Stalemate	...	.22	Stalemate	...	.22	Stalemate	...
M+9	.37	Stalemate	...	.38	Stalemate	...	.39	Stalemate	...
M+14[c]	.51	Breakthrough	26	.53	Breakthrough	18	.55	Breakthrough	17
M+120[c]	.56	Breakthrough	13	.60	Breakthrough	12	.62	Breakthrough	11
Saudi Arabia									
M+90	.75	Breakthrough	10	.93	Breakthrough	6	.97	Breakthrough	4
Korea									
M+90	.30	Stalemate	...	.32	Stalemate	...	.34	Stalemate	...

Source: Authors' estimates based on calculations described in appendix C.
a. Index of the attacker's lethality relative to the defender. Stalemate occurs when the index is in favor of the defender (at or below .50). A lower index indicates that the defender would possess the wherewithal to mount a counterattack. A higher index indicates that the attacker would break through.
b. M-day is the day the attacker begins to mobilize.
c. Details of the M+120 case can be found in table C-5.

reduced by 25 percent when it is supplied and maintained by reserve combat-service-support units. A reserve division has 75 percent of the combat power of an active-duty division and half the effectiveness when supplied and maintained by active-duty combat-service-support units. Its effectiveness decreases by another 25 percent when associated with reserve tactical support units.

In case 2, it is assumed that a reserve combat division has only half the combat power of an active-duty division and that reserve tactical support units perform at only 50 percent of their potential effectiveness; the effectiveness of combat divisions associated with these units declines commensurately.

In case 3, the combat power of the divisions does not change, since it is difficult to believe that an average reserve division-equivalent would have less than 50 percent of the firepower of an active-duty division. But reserve combat-service-support units associated with active-duty divisions operate at only 25 percent of their potential capacity and, because so many of them are only cadre units and lack experience, do even worse when supporting reserve divisions.

In all cases, the combat power and effectiveness assigned to Warsaw Pact reserve divisions are held constant: category II divisions are assumed to possess 75 percent of the combat power and effectiveness of category I divisions, while category III divisions are degraded by 50 percent in both measures.

What happens when the ground forces, allocated according to the assumptions in table 7-5, perform based on the assumptions made in table 7-6? The results are decidedly mixed (see table 7-7). In Central Europe, NATO continues to do well in resisting an attack by the Warsaw Pact at M + 4 (four days after Pact mobilization begins) in all three cases simply because the forces involved are all active-duty and host-nation support is assumed to operate at full capacity. If the Pact attacks at M + 9, the stalemate holds, although a slight increase occurs in its relative lethality because of the lesser performance of U.S. reserve combat-service-support units. But at both M + 14 and M + 120, perhaps the two most plausible of current NATO contingencies, the Pact begins to see a large enough increase in its relative lethality to have some confidence of achieving a breakthrough. Admittedly, the Pact's advantage in lethality at M + 14 makes the prospects of a NATO collapse more hypothetical than real, since the expected penetration of allied defenses could take up to three weeks or more, during which time the United States and its allies might be able to bring in enough reinforcements to plug the gap.

A large Pact buildup followed by an attack on Central Europe at $M + 120$ would present a problem of quite a different order. To deal with it, the United States would have to rely heavily on its reserves (ten divisions and comparable amounts of combat service support), as would its allies, and if its other forces were deployed as assumed in table 7-5, it would have little or nothing left to prevent the Pact from making steady advances. In any event, since a Pact breakthrough could be expected to take less than two weeks (in case 2), little time would be left to move in reinforcements, even if there were reinforcements to deploy.

The prospects in Saudi Arabia would be even worse. Because so much of the force there would be made up of reservists, a Soviet attack would be virtually impossible to contain and (in case 2) a breakthrough would probably occur after roughly six days of intensive combat. Only in Korea, despite a slight decline in the index of U.S. and allied lethality, would the military situation remain stable, largely because of the size of the South Korean forces and their strong defensive positions.

Although the number of contingencies postulated in the foregoing analysis may seem excessive, they do constitute the basis of U.S. force planning. In that planning, Army reserve forces, both combat and combat-service-support, have prominent roles to play at the very outset of a major U.S. deployment to one or more overseas theaters. And under the assumptions summarized in table 7-6, their performance makes a difference in the ability of the United States to reach its initial goal of containing enemy attacks.

Even when the reserve components are credited with quite reasonable performance (as in case 2, table 7-6), considering the equipment and the amount of training they receive, the forces fail to stalemate their attackers in three of the six contingencies considered (as seen in table 7-7). In fact, all other things being equal except for the National Guard and Reserve, if the Warsaw Pact were to begin an attack on West Germany at $M + 4$, and the two belligerents were to reinforce their combatants following the schedules postulated in table 7-3, NATO would run some risk of a collapse within about two weeks and would face an even graver crisis after little more than four months. U.S. performance would be equally poor if the Soviets were to move unopposed into Iran and then launch an attack on the Arabian peninsula. Only in South Korea would the prospects for a solid defense look promising under these rather demanding conditions.

To describe the future this grimly is not to suggest that if only the National Guard and Reserve could be made to play their roles to the hilt (and with little in the way of rehearsal), a stable military situation would loom large on the horizon. All other things are not equal. Even if the reserve components were to fulfill the most optimistic expectations for them, such other weaknesses as inadequate long-range transportation, shortages of close air support aircraft and possibly of war reserve stocks, problems with the reserve structures of the NATO allies, and insufficient emphasis on well-prepared defensive positions in Central Europe would go a long way toward crippling any U.S. effort to deal with more than one fairly large contingency. As a consequence, action on a number of bread-and-butter programs will have to be started or continued if current U.S. planning objectives are to be taken seriously.

That much said, there is not much doubt that those objectives call for fully supported, equipped, and trained ground forces in the range of thirty-eight to forty U.S. divisions (including three to four in the Marine Corps). Under present conditions the reserve components, together with existing active-duty ground forces, have the necessary structures (if not the necessary personnel) to provide that number of divisions. Whether the reserves can be converted into a rapidly deployable and fully effective fighting and tactical support force—and at what cost—is another matter. Certainly their upgrading remains an option, but not the only option, worth consideration.

CHAPTER EIGHT

CHOICES

DESPITE the higher funding it received during the 1980s, the Army is in an awkward position. By heeding its political masters' requests to prepare for everything, it is not able to do a great deal of any one thing. Because so many assets are in the reserve components, it is not in particularly good shape to execute a worldwide "strategic concept" of multiple contingencies in Europe, Asia, and the Caribbean. Yet neither is it well postured to use its active-duty forces to deal rapidly with a single but significant threat. Although those forces contain the equivalent of at least eighteen combat divisions, the combat service support for them—counting potential host-nation support and foreign civilians working indirectly for the Army—could probably sustain no more than ten to twelve divisions for more than a week and then only if current active unit assignments are rearranged.

The Army's difficulties are not all of its own making. Though not a stepchild of the armed forces, it is the least favored of the three main services when peacetime annual budgets are prepared. Over the first seven years of the Reagan administration, for example, it received only about 25 percent of the defense budget, while about 34 percent went to the Navy and 32 percent to the Air Force.[1] It suffers the further misfortune that it depends on the Air Force for much of its close air support and for most of its intercontinental and intratheater airlift, and on the Navy for sealift. Both capabilities are crucial to the Army's success, yet neither ranks very high on the priority lists of its sister services. As a result, the Army plans to have more units ready for early deployment than the Navy and Air Force can transport.

Even if defense funds were reallocated, though, certain problems

1. *Department of Defense Annual Report to the Congress, Fiscal Year 1988*, p. 326; and *Fiscal Year 1989*, p. 298.

unique to the Army would remain. Despite the examples of Korea and now Iraq, the Army still seems reluctant to lobby as hard as it might for full-scale prepared defenses in Europe. More important, under the Reagan blueprint for rearming America, the Army preferred modernizing its equipment to expanding its active-duty forces. Consequently, its dependence on the National Guard and Reserve has continued to grow. As indicated in chapter 2, more than half of the Total Army is in the Selected Reserve components. Even more striking, 70 percent of the tactical support personnel—the people who supply and maintain the combat units—are now in the National Guard and Reserve, even though less than 43 percent of the combat division personnel are reservists (see table 2-3).

Such a degree of dependence would not be a source of concern if the reserve components came close to matching their active-duty counterparts in capability and readiness. But they do not. As indicated in chapter 6, many of the units lack full sets of equipment; much of the materiel is not up-to-date; and many of the items are "borrowed" from time to time to provide emergency military assistance for other countries. Training days for the reserves are, naturally, far fewer than for the regulars, and the training itself is less demanding. It is doubtful that even the priority reserve combat units designated to round out active-duty divisions could be ready for deployment in fewer than thirty days. The consequences, as explained in the last chapter, are that reserve units—whether for combat or tactical support—might fail to meet their planned schedules in the event of a worldwide U.S. deployment and that, when they do arrive, might lack the effectiveness necessary to enable the United States to reach its initial defense objectives even if all the other conditions of success are present.

No doubt some of the equipment and manning deficiencies in the reserve components can be made up by a further infusion of resources. Yet several obstacles would remain. In principle, and at a cost, training days for reservists could be increased. Unfortunately, however, there seems to be an inverse correlation between the amount of time demanded of the reservists and their willingness (for quite understandable reasons) to remain in the reserves. Of equal import, there is a history of presidential reluctance to call up the reserves—even those that can be summoned without resort to a declaration of a national emergency. Some have gone as far as to suggest that the Army has deliberately made itself heavily dependent on the reserves to ensure that any large future commitment of U.S. ground forces overseas will trigger a call-up, an act that a prudent president would not undertake without widespread public support. Whether or not this is the case, the situation as it stands can hardly be called ideal.

Rhetoric and reality appear to be drifting ever more widely apart. Rhetoric shouts about the renewed importance of conventional forces, but the Army remains at the bottom of the budgetary totem pole. Rhetoric spotlights worldwide U.S. interests and the threat of global war, yet the Army is incapable of conducting simultaneous large-scale campaigns. With some reposturing, the Army could probably fight a war on the scale of Korea or Vietnam; it is not now in a position to provide the thirty-five or thirty-six divisions needed to deal simultaneously with contingencies in Europe, the Persian Gulf, Korea, and the Caribbean while also standing guard in Iceland, Alaska, and the Panama Canal—at least, not against enemies who are able to mobilize rapidly and put combat-ready forces into the field on relatively short notice.

Past administrations have managed to live with these gaps between rhetoric and reality, and future ones may choose to follow that course, either in the bliss of ignorance or with fingers firmly but secretly crossed. Alternatively, they may want to know what policy choices they have. Essentially, four options appear to be open to them. First, they can allow the Army to continue its heavy dependence on the reserves but modify both the programs for the reserve components and the threat assumptions. Second, they can enlarge the active-duty Army and return the reserves to their traditional role as later-arriving or follow-on backups to the deployed forces. Third, while maintaining eighteen division-equivalents in the active-duty forces, they can persuade NATO allies to bear a larger share of the burden and thereby reduce the Army's dependence on the reserves. Fourth, they can change the strategic concept in such a way as to reduce the demands on the Army, and at the same time minimize any dependence on the National Guard and Reserve for a minimum of four or five months.

Option One: Adopt More Realistic Planning Assumptions

It may seem paradoxical, after we have questioned the usefulness of the reserve components under the present strategic concept, to suggest that it makes sense to continue relying so heavily on them. Yet under certain conditions that course is reasonable. Although force planners focus on attacks within a few days or weeks of mobilization and deployment, serious questions exist as to how rapidly the Soviet armed forces can set themselves up for one or more large military operations. The questions arise because the Soviet army has to struggle with many of the same problems faced by the U.S. Army. Although Soviet ground forces allegedly consist of 209 divisions, only about 53 of them are classified category I, or combat-ready in the same sense as U.S. active-duty divisions. The remainder, like U.S. reserve forces, lack full complements of personnel, have older equipment, and in some cases are probably short of trucks, tracked vehicles, artillery, and other weapons. Moreover, the reservists who would fill out the category II and III divisions undergo little or no training. Consequently, in contrast to the contingencies postulated by U.S. force planners, it is quite plausible to suppose that the Soviet marshals would need some months, rather than a few weeks, to mobilize, organize, and make ready the ground forces for one or more major offensives.

Under current planning assumptions and despite these problems, not only are the Red ground forces allowed to attack with a minimum of warning, but the offensive unfolds pretty much as a bolt out of the political blue; no great dispute, no growing confrontation, no period of crisis precedes the assault. And that indeed may be the way in which a future war would begin. However, the greater probability is that a major crisis would precede an attack and that the Soviet Union would need some months to prepare for its offensive and to bring its East European cohorts into line. For the United States and its allies this would mean a substantial amount of warning and, given a prompt response (usually, but not always, a question mark), enough time to call up the reserves and bring them to a fighting pitch.

Obviously risks are involved in relaxing assumptions about warning, mobilization, and deployment times. History is replete with surprise attacks, although the surprise is more often tactical than strategic. And even with additional time to get the reserves in shape, further costs would be involved. At a minimum, $13 billion would be needed to correct the shortfalls in National Guard and Reserve equipment alone; costs would be substantially higher to equip the reserves with top-of-the-line weapon systems. Still, hedges against surprise attack already exist in current NATO deployments in Germany and Korea. More can be added if the Army were to reorganize its active-duty forces and depend on them for early reinforcement. In these circumstances, reserve components would deploy as a second echelon, probably at a date at least as early as that when Soviet and other category III divisions would arrive in the war zone, assuming that the Soviet forces could even get there while under heavy allied air attack.

Option Two: Increase Active Forces

A second option would be to reduce dependence on the reserves and increase the active-duty Army from eighteen to twenty-eight divisions while still keeping the current strategic concept. Such a change, which would still leave a deficit of nearly eight divisions, would require greater pressure on allies in Europe and Asia to contribute more to the common defense, especially additional ground forces. It would also add to the cost of U.S. ground forces, though the increment might not be much greater than what it would take to modernize and improve the reserves. Much would depend on the personnel increase needed to create another ten divisions with their support, which could amount to between about 270,000 and 317,000 additional troops, eventually adding between $18 billion and $21 billion a year (in fiscal 1987 dollars) to the Army's budget.[2]

Assuming that the powers that be would accede to a manpower increase of this size, the Army might try to obtain it in one of two ways. First, it could revive some form of conscription or national service.

---

2. The current combination of active-duty and reserve Army forces, with just over 1.1 million men and women deployed, yields a division slice of slightly more than 40,000 people, if only twenty-eight divisions are counted. However, the combat component of the division force turns out to be very large indeed, consisting of more than 24,000 people, whereas the tactical support, theater, and mobility forces that help to supply and maintain them average only 16,000 per division force (or 19,000 when host-nation support in Germany and South Korea are included).

Of course, another way to look at this distribution is to consider a combat division as comprising roughly 19,000 people and that the support per division averages between 12,000 and 13,000 people, with 60 percent of the division force in divisions and 40 percent in supply and maintenance (not including host-nation support). This would mean that the current total force (active and reserve) consists of the requisite 35 2/3 divisions. Thus, if one were to follow these counting rules, at least another 317,000 people would have to be added to the Army in order to produce ten more division forces of about the same size and composition. If the combat division were reduced to its more traditional size of 16,000, however, the additional personnel to obtain the same ratio of combat to support would amount to roughly 271,000. Costs are based on the assumption, derived from planning factors, that a soldier, fully capitalized, costs $67,000 a year.

There is, however, very little prospect that peacetime conscription or mandatory national service would be adopted before the occurrence of an emergency far greater than any that now exists, or is on the horizon. And the problems of the peacetime Army are unlikely to exert much influence on the short-term perspectives of national politicians. Indeed, should an emergency arise, and these perspectives change, it would almost certainly be too late for conscription to satisfy the near-term needs of the Army. By the time the selective service system could be implemented, the training infrastructure set up, and draftees put through the minimum training of roughly thirteen weeks to produce a basic infantryman and even longer to produce a specialist or technician, the National Guard and Reserve should be at least as ready to provide the combat and combat-service-support functions that, in a worldwide conflict, the Army would find in such short supply.

Alternatively, it could substitute civilians for active-duty soldiers assigned to nondeploying general support activities in the United States. As table 2-3 reflected, in fiscal 1987 there were about 200,000 such positions. If the bulk of these billets could be filled by civilians, the Army would need only about a 10 percent increase in active-duty strength to create ten new division forces. A change in the structure of the Army, however, with a greater reliance on civilians for the conduct of auxiliary and support activities would meet with substantial opposition. These activities include intelligence, research and development, communications, base operations, central logistics, management headquarters, and support installations. The Army might well feel that additional civilian substitution would cause it to lose influence over critical decisions in the interservice arena, diminish responsiveness to the needs of the combat arms, and provide fewer career opportunities for its officer corps. Perhaps equally important, the tradition that a senior officer should obtain a wide-ranging knowledge of his service and give at least the appearance of being a jack of all trades would be violated. More and more the generalist so prized by the services would be replaced by the military specialist.

The gains, in any event, might not seem worth the high costs of such a change. Admittedly, the Army would obtain 10 more division-equivalents, but the total of 28 would still fall short of the 35 2/3 calculated as necessary for the eventuality of a worldwide deployment. Moreover, the 28 divisions would be somewhat smaller than the standard Army heavy divisions, and they would be light on tactical support, requiring a continued if greatly lessened dependence on an early deployment of reserve components. Greater specialization and professionalism, fewer permanent changes of station, less turbulence in units, and a larger, ready, active-duty force capable of responding quickly to overseas emergencies would no doubt have their attractions. But it is doubtful that they would be enough to overcome traditions, costs, and the routines of what is essentially a peacetime Army.

Option Three: Depend More on Allies

A third option would not entail any incremental cost and might gain a great deal more potential support in the United States. Its feasibility, however, is bound to be in question. At issue in this option is not the strategic concept but the way in which it is carried out. U.S. force planning would continue to be based on the more or less simultaneous occurrence of three major and several minor contingencies. The active-duty Army would remain at eighteen division force equivalents, instead of the twenty-eight in the second option. But the initial contribution of U.S. ground forces to the common defense would be fixed at lower levels than is now the case. Under these conditions the reserve components would not play any part in early U.S. deployments.

To understand why this proposal differs from the second option, several aspects of U.S. force planning need to be recalled. To begin with, despite a widespread view to the contrary, no strong connection exists between U.S. interests and treaty commitments on the one hand and the U.S. strategic concept on the other. Interests may define what are seen as the conditions of U.S. economic, political, and military security. Treaties constitute both a recognition of those conditions and an agreement on how to maintain them. The strategic concept, by contrast, considers a combination of commitments, threats, capabilities, and costs as the basis for determining how the United States should respond to a major deterioration in the international situation. That the United States has explicit or implicit commitments to Latin America, Canada, Western Europe, the Middle East, Thailand, Taiwan, South Korea, Japan, and Australia does not mean either that all these regions would be threatened simultaneously or that the United States should dispose its forces on such a basis. To the contrary, force planning must and does concentrate on how, most efficiently, to deal with the specific threats that could arise more or less simultaneously in areas of importance to the United States.

Given this approach to force planning, and contrary to a widely expressed comment, there is no particular need to tailor commitments to capabilities or capabilities to overall commitments; indeed, since the introduction of more or less systematic force planning to the Pentagon, this tailoring of commitments to capabilities and vice versa has never been done. During the Kennedy and Johnson administrations, the Defense Department planned its forces on the basis of having to deal more or less simultaneously with major attacks in Europe and Asia and a minor contingency in the Caribbean. President Nixon, as a result of the widening Sino-Soviet split, decided to drop one major contingency from the force planning concept and reduce U.S. conventional forces accordingly, influenced in part, no doubt, by budgetary considerations and the shift from conscription to the all-volunteer force. Presidents Ford and Carter both went along with planning for one major and one minor contingency. President Carter tried, unsuccessfully, to withdraw the single remaining U.S. division from South Korea and reduce the American involvement there. Even before that ill-starred attempt, successive oil shocks had made the Persian Gulf an area of increasing concern, and James R. Schlesinger, while secretary of defense, not only foresaw the need for a more ambitious planning concept, but also set out to restore the size of the active-duty Army to sixteen divisions (it had fallen to about thirteen as the withdrawal from Vietnam proceeded). In the late 1970s Harold Brown continued these endeavors, and President Carter, by 1980, had declared the freedom of the Persian Gulf states a matter of vital interest to the United States. The stage was then set for a return to the planning concept of the mid-1960s.

The Reagan administration distanced itself publicly from this kind of approach to force planning and talked in general terms about preparing for a worldwide war. It seems safe to assume, however, that the Joint Chiefs of Staff and the Army not only continued to do their force planning in relation to specific contingencies, but also recognized that the Persian Gulf and the Caribbean (or, more precisely, Cuba and Nicaragua) had effectively been added to Europe and Korea as theaters in which they might be called upon to operate in the event of a major emergency.

At the same time, despite these permutations in planning for the big conventional war, the trend of conflict has gone in a different direction since the Second World War. Limited wars were reinvented and fought in Korea and Vietnam; a small engagement redolent of colonial days took place over the Falkland Islands; insurgencies, counterinsurgencies, and terrorism gained popularity around the world. To many, these have now become the military realities of the postwar world, yet uncertainty necessarily remains as to whether they constitute the wave of the future or the artifacts of the past. A prognosis of continued "small" wars certainly has recent history on its side. The only difficulties with it are that these kinds of clashes continue to be likely only so long as other military avenues—both nuclear and conventional—remain blocked, and that accidents leading to big wars can always happen. Dramatic changes in U.S. force planning therefore cannot be said to be without risk.

To say this, however, is not to argue that the force planning concept should remain immune to change. In the past, the U.S. approach was to treat allied military inputs as given—fixed and not subject to increase. U.S. forces were then calculated as the amount necessary to achieve the initial objective of containing the enemy attack. Thus if the force goal for this purpose were sixty-three divisions in Central Europe, and the allies had forty divisions available, the United States would plan on providing another twenty-three to make up the difference.

Obviously this approach could be reversed. That is to say, if the goal for the defense of Central Europe were to remain at sixty-three divisions by M + 120, the United States could explicitly agree to provide, say, a total of twelve—to be deployed within a period of several weeks—assuming a rapid mobilization and deployment by the Warsaw Pact, and the allies would agree to make up any difference then and thereafter until such time as the U.S. reserve components were combat ready and deployable. In other words, the U.S. commitment would become the constant, and allied forces would constitute the variable.

An illustration of such an approach (involving four Marine divisions as well as eighteen Army division-equivalents) is shown in table 8-1. Existing active-duty ground forces (and one reserve Marine Corps division allegedly kept at a high state of readiness) would be prepared to respond to the same number of contingencies as before. However, in Europe, the Persian Gulf, and South Korea, the allies would be expected to provide nearly eighteen more divisions of U.S. size and quality in order to replace early-deploying but inadequately trained and equipped U.S. reserve components.[3]

---

3. At some risk, this process of substitution, while taking a different form, could be carried still further. If the United States and its allies were to expand dramatically their

Table 8-1. An Alternative Distribution of U.S.–Ally Ground Force Responsibilities
Number of division-equivalents

Theater	United States	Allies	Total
North Norway	. . .	5	5
Central Europe	12	$50\frac{2}{3}$ [a]	$62\frac{2}{3}$
Thrace	. . .	4	4
Saudi Arabia	$6\frac{1}{3}$	$2\frac{2}{3}$ [b]	9
Korea	1	23 [c]	24
Caribbean	$1\frac{2}{3}$	. . .	$1\frac{2}{3}$
Iceland	$\frac{1}{3}$	. . .	$\frac{1}{3}$
Alaska	$\frac{1}{3}$	. . .	$\frac{1}{3}$
Panama Canal	$\frac{1}{3}$	. . .	$\frac{1}{3}$
Total	22 [d]	$85\frac{1}{3}$	$107\frac{1}{3}$

Source: Authors' estimates.
a. Allies would have to add $16\frac{2}{3}$ divisions to their current total (estimated at 34 divisions).
b. Saudi Arabia and Jordan would be expected to contribute these forces.
c. South Korea would add 2 divisions to its current total of 21.
d. U.S. total includes 4 Marine Corps divisions (3 active and 1 reserve).

Objections to this option would obviously exist. If, as part of the arrangement, resources were either frozen or reduced for the reserves on the ground that they would revert to their traditional role of being a long-term backup force, protests no doubt would be heard both from Congress and from the reserve organizations themselves. More important, the stakes would change in the perennial issue of whether the allies would pick up the slack in ground forces left by the reduced U.S. commitment. Efforts dating back a quarter of a century have persuaded them to make only modest improvements in these capabilities. In effect, they have bet that the combination of the U.S. nuclear umbrella, however porous, and the U.S. determination to keep them out of hostile hands would save them the costs of any substantial military buildup. There is

synthetic oil capacities, they (and particularly the United States) could reduce substantially ground and other forces earmarked for the Persian Gulf, and the trade of military for oil capability could probably be made at zero cost. Admittedly, the synthetic fuel would not be competitive in the current marketplace. But to the extent that the U.S. interest in the Gulf derives from oil, an investment in synthetic fuel production would be at least as good an investment in national security as the forces earmarked for the Central Command, which has the Persian Gulf as its principal theater of operations. A difficulty does occur, however, in connection with such a trade. It might effectively hand over access to Persian Gulf oil to the Soviet Union if its leaders chose to exercise their military power in the region. And it could also fulfill the long-term Russian ambition of obtaining warm water ports in the Gulf, although the short-term importance of such an acquisition has probably been exaggerated, given the poor lines of communication between the Trans-Caucasus and the Gulf and the time and cost it would take to upgrade them.

no certainty that a reduced U.S. military commitment would change their bet. And the danger looms that, if they did take the United States seriously, they would move increasingly to improve their nuclear rather than their conventional capabilities. It is the prospect of these possibilities that has led the United States to avoid a showdown over how to share the burdens of the common defense, particularly since the U.S. burden in any particular region except the Persian Gulf is not any heavier than that of its allies.

Option Four: Limit U.S. Military Objectives

One fact about the need for conventional forces is clear, however. Were it not for the Soviet Union and its large conventional capabilities, U.S. Army active-duty ground forces (somewhat differently organized and with the assurance of host-nation support in West Germany and South Korea) should be able to respond adequately to any challenge from another country without any early dependence on either the reserve components or some form of peacetime conscription. Thus, how many ground forces are enough depends critically on the intentions as well as the capabilities of the Soviet Union. As already noted, severe limitations exist on the ability of the Soviets rapidly to mobilize and deploy massive ground forces. Equally important, at least for the short run, the current Soviet leadership appears to be more interested in domestic reform than in foreign adventure and would welcome some respite from the arms competition. Arguably, the United States need no longer hedge against the possibility of World War III, whatever the efforts of the past, in which case the limitations of the Army reserves would not loom large. Indeed, if this strategic concept was adopted, the growing dependence on the reserves could be safely curtailed.

The Real Choices

Unfortunately, however, the size and composition of U.S. and allied ground forces cannot depend on short-run considerations, especially when the Soviet army continues to number about two million men. President Gorbachev may indeed be well intentioned. But in the process, he is creating a revolution of rising expectations in the Soviet Union as well as parts of Eastern Europe. Suppose that, for whatever reasons, he is slow to meet those expectations, the level of discontent increases and another uprising occurs in Eastern Europe, the Red Army begins brutally to put it down, and NATO in outrage begins to contemplate retaliation.

Such a turn of events is not impossible, nor can one rule out in these circumstances what amounts to an unintended clash between East and West. Whether it could be controlled or would expand is uncertain. About all one can say is that a worldwide conflagration cannot be ruled out, however low its probability may seem today.

Thus if insurance still seems warranted, there is no obvious way for the United States to obtain it on acceptable terms except by some continued dependence on the National Guard and Reserve. Peacetime revival of conscription does not seem to have a chance politically. Some form of national service might have somewhat higher odds, but its functions have not yet been well defined, its costs would be high, and there is little assurance that the Army would gain any additional qualified recruits from the process. As for our allies, the prospects are dim that they would fill the gap caused by any retrenchment of U.S. military commitments to the common defense. Doubts are in order, in fact, that they will be willing to make the more modest effort necessary to reach the goals of the ideal or baseline force outlined in chapter 7. Expanding and restructuring the Army by assigning more of its support activities to the civilian sector would plug part but not all of the gap between goals and means, but implementation would be costly and the Army itself would almost certainly resist leaving to civilians positions of influence within the Army itself and within the interservice arena.

What, then, do the choices come down to in the end? When all is said and done, only two seem feasible for the foreseeable future. The first, option four above, is to bet on a continued era of limited wars, small-scale engagements, and what euphemistically is called low-intensity conflict. Such a bet would mean keeping the active-duty forces at their present size and composition, relying on them exclusively to conduct the initial stages of all overseas operations, and ending their early dependence on reserve components for round-out units, augmentation, and combat service support. The National Guard and Reserve would continue to exist at current levels of manning, equipment, and training. But no one would expect them to serve any purpose other than their historical role: insurance against a large, long war in which the time would be available to correct their deficiencies and bring them to an acceptable level of combat effectiveness.

The second choice, option one above, is to continue to bet on worldwide instability and to prepare for and hope to deter a war of multiple contingencies and theaters. This approach could still make the active-duty Army, through rearrangements in its support structure, less dependent on the reserves for its initial operations than is now the case. At the same time, it would entail a more systematic, higher-priority, and more dedicated effort to overcome the seemingly inherent obstacles to improving the readiness and effectiveness of the reserve components.

As a first step in this direction, the Army would have to provide more modern equipment to both combat and combat-service-support units to the tune of $17 billion or more. These costs need not be viewed as incremental increases in defense spending. Because of the way in which the United States has conducted its most recent defense expansion, inefficiencies continue to abound and some of them are still reversible. Many programs are sufficiently early in their development so that opportunities remain to cut back or cancel them. The Stealth bomber, the MX missile, the small ICBM, the strategic defense initiative, and the Seawolf attack submarine—not to mention various advanced tactical fighters—represent a small sample of the available possibilities. Despite expected future constraints on U.S. defense budgets, savings from these and other programs would suffice to pay for improvements in the Army, whatever the option for restructuring it has chosen.[4]

Second, the Army must seek to improve reserve training, not by adding more hours (which may be counterproductive, as indicated in chapter 6), but by adopting more realistic readiness goals and an integrated training strategy that exploits emerging training technologies. In this regard, the Army reserves should not be counted on to achieve readiness higher than company-level, leaving to active-duty units of battalion-size or larger the higher states of readiness needed for early deployment.

Third, the Army should make the provision of federal funds dependent on the progress of reserve components in improving and maintaining agreed standards of readiness and deployability. Fourth, and in that same connection, the secretary of defense should undertake an independent review of existing force planning contingencies and determine not only the size and composition of the U.S. ground forces that will be needed but also the times, realistically, at which they will be needed. If

4. For a fuller discussion of these possibilities, see William W. Kaufmann, "A Defense Agenda for Fiscal Years 1990–1994," in John D. Steinbruner, ed., *Restructuring American Foreign Policy* (Brookings, 1989), chap. 3.

he finds that the Soviet capacity for rapid mobilization and deployment has been exaggerated, and thus that current deployment schedules are unrealistically demanding for the active-duty forces (despite POMCUS and airlift) and *completely* beyond the reach of the reserve components, and that less hectic responses are in order, then it is conceivable, even given existing constraints, that the reserve components can actually play the role the Army should assign to them.

Perhaps it is too optimistic to believe that a new force planning concept can be developed that is realistic about what the Soviet Union can do and at the same time does not require most U.S. reserve components to mobilize within thirty days or deploy within ninety days of a Pact mobilization. But the time has certainly come to bring the rhetoric of the Total Army into conformity with what the reserve components are capable of doing. Where U.S. ground forces are concerned the country currently has a three-to-four contingency rhetoric and a one-contingency capability.

Some may argue that the mix is about right for current conditions. But if one seriously believes that hedges against low-probability events such as worldwide conflict are worth acquiring if the price is not too high, then somehow the capability must be brought more in tune with the rhetoric. At present, only the Army National Guard and Reserve offer an opportunity to near that goal, especially if the reality is somewhat less threatening than the standard rhetoric would have the nation believe. Even then, the Army will have to believe far more in the Total Army and work much harder than is now the case to make the reserve components a more integral part of the total.

MOBILIZATION AUTHORITY

	Situation[a]		
Item	Operational mission requiring augmentation of active force	Contingency operation, war plan, national emergency (partial mobilization)	War or national emergency (total mobilization)
Action required	Presidential executive order	Presidential proclamation of a national emergency and an executive order.	Passage of a public law or joint resolution by Congress declaring war or national emergency.
Authority	10 U.S.C. 673b P.L. 99-661 (amending P.L. 96-584)	10 U.S.C. 673a	10 U.S.C. 671a 10 U.S.C. 672
Personnel involved	Units and individuals of Selected Reserve; limited to 200,000 (all services) for up to 90 days, or for up to 180 days if the president deems necessary.	Ready Reserve units and Individual Ready Reserve; limited to 1,000,000 (all services) for up to two years.	National Guard and Reserve units, Individual Ready Reserve, Standby Reserve, members of Retired Reserve. No numerical or time limitation unless established by Congress.
Remarks	President must report to Congress within 24 hours on circumstances and anticipated use of forces. May not be used in lieu of a call-up (10 U.S.C. 331 et seq., 3500, 8500), or for disaster relief.	Presidents may extend appointments, enlistments, and periods of service when Congress is not in session. 10 U.S.C. 671b.	May extend enlistments in Regular and Reserve forces and extend period of active service for duration of the war plus six months.

Source: Adapted from U.S. Army War College, *Army Command and Management: Theory and Practice* (Carlisle Barracks, Penn., 1985–86), p. 13-16.
  a. Does not include mobilizations for domestic purposes, which are covered under other statutes.

ILLUSTRATIVE DEPLOYMENT
SEQUENCE FOR NATO

Army combat unit[a]	Day required in theater	Remarks
Forward deployed		
1st Armored Division	In place	. . .
3d Armored Division	In place	. . .
3d Infantry Division (Mech)	In place	. . .
8th Infantry Division (Mech)	In place	. . .
3d Brigade, 1st Infantry Division (Mech)	In place	. . .
Brigade, 2d Armored Division	In place	. . .
Brigade, 1st Cavalry Division	In place	. . .
2d Armored Cavalry Regiment	In place	. . .
11th Armored Cavalry Regiment	In place	. . .
Augmentation and reinforcement		
1st Cavalry Division (2/3)	M + 2	. . .
2d Armored Division (2/3)	M + 2	. . .
1st Infantry Division (Mech) (2/3)	M + 2	. . .
24th Infantry Division (Mech) (2/3)	M + 2	Guard round-out brigade to follow
3d Armored Cavalry Regiment	M + 2	. . .
4th Infantry Division (Mech) (3/3)	M + 4	. . .
5th Infantry Division (Mech) (2/3)	M + 4	Guard round-out brigade to follow
9th Infantry Division	M + 11	. . .
6th Combat Brigade (Air Cavalry)	M + 12	. . .
101st Airborne Division (Air Assault)	M + 13	. . .
197th Infantry Brigade	M + 13	. . .
2d Infantry Division (Mech)	M + 16	. . .
194th Armored Brigade	M + 22	. . .
82d Airborne Division	M + 24	. . .
7th Infantry Division	M + 25	Guard round-out brigade to follow
32d Infantry Brigade (Mech)	M + 28	Guard augmentation unit
67th Infantry Brigade (Mech)	M + 28	Guard augmentation unit
81st Infantry Brigade (Mech)	M + 29	Guard augmentation unit
256th Infantry Brigade (Mech)	M + 29	Guard round-out to 5th Infantry Division

Continued on next page

Army combat unit[a]	Day required in theater	Remarks
48th Infantry Brigade (Mech)	M + 29	Guard round-out to 24th Infantry Division
39th Infantry Brigade	M + 29	Guard augmentation unit
41st Infantry Brigade	M + 30	Guard round-out to 7th Infantry Division
53d Infantry Brigade	M + 40	Guard separate unit (Canal Zone)
187th Infantry Brigade	M + 40	Reserve separate unit (Iceland)
30th Infantry Brigade	M + 40	Guard separate unit
205th Infantry Brigade (Light)	M + 40	Reserve separate unit (Alaska)
116th Armored Cavalry Regiment	M + 40	Guard separate unit
45th Infantry Brigade	M + 40	Guard separate unit
58th Infantry Brigade	M + 54	Guard separate unit
69th Infantry Brigade	M + 54	Guard separate unit
116th Infantry Brigade	M + 56	Guard separate unit
40th Infantry Division (Mech)	M + 57	Guard division
50th Armored Division	M + 60	Guard division
26th Infantry Division	M + 60	Guard division
49th Armored Division	M + 66	Guard division
30th Armored Brigade	M + 70	Guard separate unit
31st Amored Brigade	M + 70	Guard separate unit
155th Armored Brigade	M + 70	Guard separate unit
157th Infantry Brigade (Mech)	M + 70	Reserve separate unit
218th Infantry Brigade (Mech)	M + 70	Guard separate unit
107th Armored Cavalry Regiment	M + 70	Guard separate unit
163d Armored Cavalry Regiment	M + 70	Guard division
38th Infantry Division	M + 72	Guard division
42d Infantry Division	M + 75	Guard division
28th Infantry Division	M + 79	Guard division

Source: Adapted from Office of the Assistant Secretary of Defense (Program Analysis and Evaluation), NATO *Center Region Military Balance Study, 1978–1984* (Department of Defense, July 1979), annex A.

a. This deployment schedule was meant to describe potential rather than actual capabilities for fiscal 1983, given the limitations of strategic lift assets.

MEASURING MILITARY PERFORMANCE

THE conclusions drawn in chapter 7 about the performance of the Army National Guard and Reserve are based on systematic methods for assessing the interaction of opposing ground and close air support forces in a military engagement. Various techniques have been developed to arrive at these particular kinds of capabilities, ranging from simple counts of numbers of troops, tanks, aircraft, and other weapons, on one extreme, to large, sophisticated war-gaming simulations, on the other. The method used here goes well beyond simple counting but stops well short of the elaborate computer-based models that claim to capture the "dynamics of combat" or predict the outcome·of future battles and campaigns. The goal here is more modest: an attempt to assess the effect of a given military capability according to a limited number of measures, on the assumption that many other factors do not favor one or the other of the belligerents. Thus the analysis deliberately omits such variables as generalship, organization, the "operational art," or the hundreds of other factors that could affect the results of a battle or campaign.

Admittedly, this approach simplifies extremely complex and inadequately understood relationships and has inherent limitations. But since no conceptually sophisticated model of conventional combat dynamics is complete or generally accepted, and since assessments of conventional force balances appear to depend more on input assumptions than on differences in the method of calculation, it seems appropriate to base these assessments on simple arithmetic that seems to have been informally institutionalized over the years. Though few Army officials would directly defend the habit, a number of assumptions that have appeared in Army manuals have been used as rules of thumb, representing the inherited wisdom of the military establishment. These have focused on the interaction of opposing military forces and on such specific results as losses of men and materiel, time, movement of the front, and penetration of defensive positions.

The informal model of force interactions embodied in the assumptions has been used by policymakers to organize their judgments in making budget and force structure decisions. By making the assumptions explicit, one can test the sensitivity of these results to changes in particular forces, their performance, and the substitution of one type of capability for another.

The results are obtained through a series of analytical steps.

1. *Aggregating disparate and heterogeneous forces into manageable and apparently comparable forces.* Military analysts traditionally have used firepower scores of various kinds to homogenize weapons of differing capabilities in order to make the assessment of large-unit actions more manageable. The Army, for example, calculates the potential combat power of a combined arms force, which until recently was called its weighted unit value (WUV), by measuring the relative value and potential effectiveness of similar weapons against a standard for their particular category (previously called a weapon effectiveness index, or WEI),[1] weighting the various categories of weapons in a given scenario and theater of operations, and aggregating across all weapons assigned to a unit.[2] Thus, by 1979 standards, the Army assigned a weighted unit value of 6,553.55 to U.S. tank battalions and 5,914.27 to infantry battalions in a defensive mode in the European theater.[3] Combat power can also be calculated for larger formations by aggregating the weighted scores for their assigned weaponry. Divisions of varying types and of

1. Although the Army has replaced the WEI/WUV methodology, it remains the only detailed information for calculating combat power that is publicly available, and it continues to be widely used in assessments of conventional forces. The new system, called "division equivalent firepower (DEF)," has been kept under wraps by the Army, but Barry Posen, a former Pentagon analyst, has suggested that the differences between the two methods are slight. Barry R. Posen, "Is NATO Decisively Outnumbered?" *International Security*, vol. 12 (Spring 1988), note 12 on pp. 190–92.

2. The standard in the small arms category in 1979, for example, was the M-16 rifle, which was assigned a weapon effectiveness index (WEI) of 1.00. Based on judgments concerning relative firepower, mobility, and survivability, the Soviet AKS-74 rifle was also assigned an index of 1.00, while the U.S. M-2 heavy machine-gun was given a value of 1.76. See U.S. Army War Gaming Directorate, *Weapon Effectiveness Indices/Weighted Unit Values* III (WEI/WUV III), CAA-SR-79-12 (Bethesda, Md.: Army Concepts Analysis Agency, reprint, November 1979), p. P-9. The small arms category, in turn, was assigned a weight of 3.7 (for units defending in Europe), compared with 94.0 for the tank category and 109.0 for attack helicopters. Ibid., p. 13–7.

3. Ibid., pp. Q-2, Q-3.

different nations can then be normalized in total scores or, as has become customary in defense analysis circles, in U.S. armored division equivalents.[4]

The combat power estimates used in chapter 7 (table 7-6) were derived from the Army's WEI/WUV data, adjusted by the authors to conform with official Department of Defense estimates of the ratio of Warsaw Pact to NATO ground force combat power.[5] Moreover, so that effectiveness (as defined below) can be treated as a separate variable, the Army's figures have been adjusted to exclude those factors that are judged by the authors to contribute more to the effectiveness with which firepower is used than to the potential firepower represented by the weapon inventory itself. Thus the combat power assigned to an average U.S. division or its equivalent is 48,000, and the power assigned to an average Soviet division-equivalent is 40,000. Similar assessments have been made for the forces of each of the belligerent nations for the scenarios described in chapter 7.

2. *Manning the front and concentrating forces.* Each side is expected to man the front on which the campaign will be fought, and to do so in sufficient density to prevent the other side from achieving an easy breakthrough. Based on an assumption that each side would have to commit just over 1 million units of combat power to cover a 700-kilometer front in Central Europe, under the M + 14 scenario the Warsaw Pact would be left with residual combat power roughly three times larger than

4. For example, William P. Mako has calculated the weighted unit value of a U.S. armored division to be 47,490 and a Soviet armored division to be 31,143. By his calculations, the Soviet division would be equivalent to about two-thirds (66 percent) of a U.S. armored division. See his *U.S. Ground Forces and the Defense of Central Europe* (Brookings, 1983), pp. 114, 121.

5. Although military analysts for more than fifty years have used firepower scores of various kinds to homogenize weapons of differing capabilities in order to make the assessment of large-unit actions more manageable, subjective elements have increasingly entered into the weighting of specific weapons and the counting of "effective" weapons, and such factors as rates of fire, weights of projectiles, accuracy, and reliability are thrown in almost indiscriminately along with other features of the weapons. Despite these problems, what is important about such scores is not so much what numerical value is given to a particular unit but whether, as one example, the ratio of Warsaw Pact to NATO ground combat power (with effectiveness factors removed from the scoring) conforms to military judgments about the ratio, and how those judgments were reached. Once that is understood, it becomes possible not only to treat effectiveness as a separate variable, but also to be quite explicit in varying the ratios. The Pentagon estimates, by a measure that includes both quantity and quality of forces, that the Warsaw Pact's advantage in in-place ground force combat power is more than 2.2 to 1. *Department of Defense Annual Report to the Congress, Fiscal Year 1988*, p. 30.

Table C-1. Order of Battle and Operating Assumptions for Hypothetical Campaign
Thousands of units of combat power unless otherwise specified

Item	Blue force	Red force
Total combat power	1,950	3,950
Less: Coverage of the front (700 km)	1,050	1,050
Equals: reserves	**900**	**2,900**
Plus: Forces on line in attack sector ($66\frac{2}{3}$ km)	100	100
Equals: combat power in attack sector	**1,000**	**3,000**
Daily effectiveness	.04	.02
Daily movement (percent of 20 km)[a]	Percent $= \exp\left(-(4/x)^2\right) \cdot 100$	
Depth of prepared defenses (km)	20	20
Level at which force will probably collapse	600	1,800
Index of relative lethality (P_D)[b]	$P_D = \dfrac{B^2 b}{B^2 b + R^2 r}$	$P_D = \dfrac{R^2 r}{R^2 r + B^2 B}$

a. Where x = ratio of combat power
b. Where B and R = combat power; and b and r = effectiveness.

NATO's.[6] It is further assumed that the Warsaw Pact concentrates in an attack sector (with a frontage of about 67 kilometers) those forces that are not manning the front, while NATO counterconcentrates its reserves on the same sector. The critical battle thus takes place in the area of concentration, where the Warsaw Pact initially enjoys a 3:1 advantage in combat power (see table C-1).

3. *Establishing levels of effectiveness for attacking and defending forces.* Measures of combat power, in themselves, do not determine the extent of damage that the combatant forces can be expected to inflict on each other. The effectiveness with which the forces employ their firepower depends on such factors as target acquisition, the probability that a weapon will be fired (which reflects training and morale), accuracy, and reliability.

Based on historical data, values can be assigned to each of these

6. Based on the military rule-of-thumb that a division frontage of 32 kilometers represents an acceptable risk, an average of 1,500 units of combat power would have to be deployed for each kilometer of front. Obviously, lower concentrations would be required in forested and urban areas and in mountainous terrain. By comparison, a Rand Corporation assessment of the conventional balance in Europe assumed that a division could cover a 25-kilometer front with a coherent defense. See James A. Thomson and Nanette C. Gantz, *Conventional Arms Control Revisited: Objectives in the New Phase*, Rand Note N-2697-AF (Santa Monica, Calif.: Rand Corp., December 1987), p. 12. For a discussion of the evaluation of division frontages, see B. H. Liddell Hart, *Deterrent or Defence: A Fresh Look at the West's Military Position* (London: Stevens and Sons, 1960), pp. 97–109.

variables and overall effectiveness expressed in terms of an index that shows the relative lethality of the two forces and is related to how each force will perform on a given day. The assigned values hinge on such factors as the mode of operation (attacking or defending and, if attacking, the type of attack) and the extent to which the position of the defender is fortified. Generally speaking, defending forces can be expected to inflict relatively more casualties on attacking forces than they themselves would take. Army planning factors, for example, assume that a division attacking an enemy position will lose 3.8 percent of its force on the first day and 1.9 percent on each succeeding day. If the defender is in a fortified zone, the figures are 6.3 and 3.2 percent, respectively. Divisions defending a position, on the other hand, are expected to take 1.9 percent casualties the first day and 1.0 percent on succeeding days.[7] Actual losses will be a function of the size of the engaged forces.

4. *Engaging the forces, establishing the losses of combat power, and moving the front.* Given the above assumptions, the consequences of an attack in the area of concentration can be traced arithmetically. What happens, quite simply, is that the combatants simultaneously shoot at each other. On the first day of the battle, the defender with a combat power of, say, 1,000 and a kill probability of 4 percent can eliminate 40 units of enemy combat power, and the attacker with a combat power of 3,000 and a kill probability of 2 percent can reduce the defender's strength by 60 units. Accordingly, as the force ratios change, the front is assumed to move at a rate dependent on the type of unit (infantry, mechanized, or armor) and terrain characteristics.[8]

Relating force ratios to advances and retreats is obviously a surrogate for more complex results. A breakthrough by the attacker could be

7. U.S. Army Command and General Staff College, *Planning Factors,* Student Text 101-2 (Ft. Leavenworth, Kan., June 1985), p. 4-27.

8. For tables that relate these factors, see Department of the Army, *Field Manual: Maneuver Control,* FM 105-5 (December 1973), appendix H. A simpler, if more aggregate, method for calculating movement of the front is provided by the equation: $y = \exp(-(4/x)^2) \times 100$, where y = percent of daily movement potential, and x = ratio of the opposing forces after a given day of fighting.

This equation is derived from the equation for the normal curve. See Frederick Mosteller, Robert E. K. Rourke, and George B. Thomas, Jr., *Probability and Statistics* (Reading, Mass.: Addison-Wesley Publishing, 1961), p. 230. This equation, it should be noted, is a refinement of the one presented in William W. Kaufmann, "Appendix: The Arithmetic of Force Planning," in John D. Steinbruner and Leon V. Sigal, eds., *Alliance Security: NATO and the No-First-Use Question* (Brookings, 1983), p. 214. The updated equation is considered a better statistical fit to Army data.

followed by an attempt to encircle and destroy a portion of the defending forces. The attack might be contained, as it usually was in the First World War, but only after the attacker had driven a salient into the defending lines. A defending commander, seeing himself suffering heavy losses and threatened by salients and the possibility of breakthroughs, might decide to retreat—not according to some formula but in order to reach a more defensible and possibly narrower front with shorter lines of communication, improved logistics, and fewer losses. He might, if allowed, make the same type of decision in order to trade space for the time necessary to obtain reinforcements and possibly prepare for a costly counteroffensive to regain the lost territory.

All of these possibilities can be explored by arithmetic or other means. Some of them, assuming a breakdown in U.S. or allied intelligence, generalship, tactics, logistics, force matchups with the enemy (allied infantry, for example, trapped by enemy tanks), could even have a major impact on U.S. force size and composition. But any effort at theater-level analysis that focuses primarily on force size and composition as the dependent variables, and at the same time attempts to make the analysis useful to senior policymakers, must engage in some heroic assumptions. Among them are the premises that the United States and its allies will make no more or no greater mistakes than the Soviet Union and its allies; that nature will treat both sides evenhandedly; that generalship, organization, and tactics will not affect the outcome; that forces from different countries, speaking different languages, and operating incompatible communications equipment can be coordinated effectively; and that enemy forces sensibly deployed and employed will be the decisive determinant of the land, air, and naval capabilities needed by the United States and its allies.

5. *Measuring the results.* Assuming a fight to the finish, the analysis determines (a) which side totally destroys the other, (b) the residual forces of the winner, and (c) the time (in days) it takes to complete the process. The methodology also permits calculations of time to penetration of prepared defenses and of unit losses (assuming a degradation of 40 percent in a given force signifies a high probability of its disintegration).[9] This approach also facilitates the calculation of an index of relative

---

9. For units on the defensive, the Army assumes that when casualties reach 40 percent, "The defending unit is totally ineffective and either must be replaced immediately or risk being overrun." Department of the Army, *Field Manual: Maneuver Control*, p. D-19.

lethality, which, as indicated, relates to the ability of one side to destroy the other and serves as a substitute for less helpful statements about "requirements" or "minimum risk" forces.[10]

Finally, whatever the attractions of trading space for time or better defensive positions (such as the Weser-Lech line or the Rhine), the United States has committed itself to a *forward defense* in several key theaters. Thus the most critical test of existing or proposed capabilities is whether they can achieve an index of relative lethality (at least 50 percent) sufficient to prevent the enemy from inflicting unacceptable losses and breaking through U.S. and allied forward defenses. The military model provides the data necessary to judge whether a given set of capabilities (including land forces, organic air defenses, and close air support aircraft) can pass these tests.

10. The index of relative lethality on a given day for Blue and Red forces, respectively, is expressed as follows:

$$\frac{B^2 b}{B^2 b + R^2 r}; \frac{R^2 r}{R^2 r + B^2 b}$$

where B and R = combat power; and b and r = combat effectiveness. See Garry D. Brewer and Martin Shubik, *The War Game: A Critique of Military Problem Solving* (Harvard University Press, 1979), pp. 77–78. Other formulations are available; see, for example, Philip M. Morse and George E. Kimball, *Methods of Operations Research*, rev. ed. (Los Altos, Calif.: Peninsula Publishing, 1970), pp. 67–71. These formulations are derived from the renowned work of Frederick William Lanchester, a pioneer in the modeling of conventional combat, and specifically from the so-called Lanchester square law. The need to put the results obtained from these particular formulae in a proper perspective cannot be overemphasized. As Morse and Kimball point out, "The results of Lanchester's equations are simply the most probable results. For the first stages of the battle there is, of course, a certain finite probability of other numbers of combatants surviving, and in the later stages of the battle the solutions to Lanchester's equations may deviate widely from the possible results. This is due to the fact that after a certain length of time there is a certain probability that all of one side will have been eliminated, and the battle will actually have been terminated before the average solution of Lanchester's equations predicts that it would end." Ibid., p. 67.

But as Morse and Kimball also note, "As long as the equations are not pressed too hard (such as by going to the limit of annihilation of one force), . . . the solutions of the equations will correspond quite closely to the 'expected value' obtained from the probability analysis. One must expect the actual results to deviate from the expected values, with the average deviation increasing as the solutions tend toward the ultimate annihilation of one force." Ibid., p. 71.

The approach used here has the advantage of conforming with the military views about the significance of force ratios, which are extensively used by the Pentagon's civilian and military force planners. See, for example, Office of the Assistant Secretary of Defense (Program Analysis and Evaluation), *NATO Center Region Military Balance Study, 1978–1984* (Department of Defense, July 1979), p. I-27.

A straightforward but more or less hypothetical example, based on the assumptions discussed above and summarized in table C-1, will show how this particular mode of analysis works. Red and Blue forces (which for simplicity consist only of ground forces) have manned a front 700 kilometers long and Red has concentrated for an attack while Blue has replied with a counterconcentration. Because of concentration, Red's advantage in combat power goes from slightly more than 2:1 overall to 3:1 in the attack sector. But because Blue's forces are on the defensive and fighting from prepared positions, they are twice as effective as Red's attacking forces.

The consequences of Red's attack in the area of concentration are traced out arithmetically in table C-2. On the first day Blue kills or otherwise disables 40 Red units (1,000 x .04), or about 1.3 percent of Red's assets, and Red disposes of 60 Blue units (3,000 x .02), or 6 percent of Blue's initial combat power. Because of resulting force ratios, the front moves nearly four kilometers, and Red now has an index of lethality relative to Blue of better than 60 percent. As shown in table C-2, by the end of the fourth day of the battle, Red has advanced a total of more than 20 kilometers and has broken through Blue's prepared defenses—all this on the assumption that neither side has yet been able to replace the losses it has suffered.[11] By the end of the seventh day, still without reinforcements, Blue's forces in the sector have fallen to less than 60 percent of their original combat power, and shortly after the end of the sixteenth day, Blue has become stretched so thin that he no longer can adequately cover the 700-kilometer front and becomes vulnerable to multiple Red attacks. After little more than eighteen days, Red has destroyed all of Blue's forces in the attack sector and advanced 227 kilometers. In short, if Blue's objective was to maintain a forward defense without any significant loss of territory, he failed miserably to do so and, depending on the criterion used, failed quite rapidly. In fact, on the average, his index of relative lethality proved to be only about 18 percent.[12] To achieve a stalemate he would have had to increase his

11. Assumptions about the depth of prepared defenses vary. A pair of Rand analysts have defined a "stalwart conventional defense line" as holding Pact forces inside the NATO main battle area, which they assumed to be 30 kilometers deep. See Thomson and Gantz, *Conventional Arms Control Revisited*, p. 7.

12. The number calculated in this example (.8189) is not strictly a statement of Red's ability to break through Blue's defenses. In fact, there is no simple formulation using force ratios for calculating the index of lethality related to a break-point; accordingly Red's average index of lethality is used as a surrogate for the probability of breakthrough.

Table C-2. Arithmetical Analysis of Hypothetical Campaign

Day	Combat power[a] Blue	Combat power[a] Red	Movement (km)	Cumulative movement (km)	Index of Red's lethality relative to Blue	Comments
0	1,000	3,000	...	...	...	
1	940	2,960	3.98	3.98	.6116	
2	881	2,922	4.67	8.65	.6238	
3	823	2,887	5.45	14.10	.6369	
4	765	2,854	6.34	20.44	.6510	Red penetrates Blue's defenses (20 km)
5	708	2,823	7.31	27.75	.6660	
6	652	2,795	8.37	36.12	.6819	
7	596	2,769	9.53	45.65	.7010	Blue at less than 60% of strength
8	541	2,745	10.74	56.39	.7173	
9	486	2,723	12.01	68.40	.7369	
10	432	2,704	13.29	81.69	.7578	
11	378	2,687	14.57	96.26	.7804	
12	324	2,672	15.81	112.07	.8048	
13	271	2,659	16.94	129.01	.8307	
14	218	2,648	17.94	146.95	.8586	
15	165	2,639	18.79	165.74	.8889	
16	112	2,632	19.43	185.17	.9216	
17	59	2,628	19.84	205.01	.9570	Porous front[b]
18	6	2,626	19.99	225.00	.9955	
18.1	0	2,626	2.00	227.00	1.0000	t_{end} and n_{end} in Lanchester format[c]
...	...	...	227.00	...	14.8217	÷ 18.1 = .8189

Source: See text.

a. Blue's effectiveness = .04; Red's effectiveness = .02.

b. When Blue's combat power drops below 100, he can no longer adequately cover the attack sector and becomes vulnerable to multiple Red attacks.

c. Defined in table C-3.

Table C-3. Lanchester Equations

1. Assumptions
   B and R = combat power
   b and r = effectiveness
   Blue is the probable winner

2. Blue's index of relative lethality
   $$P_D = \frac{B^2 b}{B^2 b + R^2 r}$$

3. Number of Blue remaining after a fight to the finish
   $$n_{end} = B \left(1 - \frac{R^2 r}{B^2 b}\right)^{1/2}$$

4. Length (in days) of a fight to the finish
   $$t_{end} = \frac{1}{(br)^{1/2}} \ln \left[\frac{(B^2 b)^{1/2} + (R^2 r)^{1/2}}{(B^2 b)^{1/2} - (R^2 r)^{1/2}}\right]^{1/2}$$

5. Number of Blue remaining at the end of a given number of days (t)
   $$B_t = \frac{\left(B - \frac{r^{1/2}}{b^{1/2}} R\right) \exp^{((rb)^{1/2} t)} + \left(B + \frac{r^{1/2}}{b^{1/2}} R\right) \exp^{(-(rb)^{1/2} t)}}{2}$$

combat power by nearly 60 percent or raise his effectiveness by a factor of 4.5.

While all of these results are a function of arithmetic, the most elementary algebra, and trial and error, it turns out that most (but not all) of the same results can essentially be duplicated with far less time and effort by the application of several equations, shown in table C-3, derived from what has come to be known as Lanchester's square law. Table C-4 compares the results of the arithmetic in table C-2 with those produced by the equations in table C-3. The arithmetic provides a somewhat richer set of results because it permits the computation of movement, whereas the Lanchester equations do not. However, the Lanchester equations, in addition to saving time, have the advantage of facilitating sensitivity tests, the substitution of one type of capability for another, and the advance determination of the changes required to increase (or decrease) to the desired level the ability to achieve a given objective such as a sustained forward defense.[13]

13. Because the Lanchester equations reproduce the results of the institutionalized arithmetic closely enough over the ratios relevant for contemporary forces, they provide a computational convenience for the purposes of simple, practical, and admittedly crude force structure assessments. The Lanchester equations, however, are not a necessity nor does their use in this manner require that Lanchester's logic be rigidly applied. For

Table C-4. Comparison of the Arithmetic with the Lanchester Solutions

	Arithmetic		Lanchester	
Item	Blue force	Red force	Blue force	Red force
Index of relative lethality	.18	.82	.18	.82
Time to penetration of prepared defenses (days)	. . .	4	a	a
Sixty percent of original combat power	600	1,800	600	1,800
Time to 60 percent (days)	7	. . .	7	. . .
Movement of front by 7th day	. . .	44.65	a	a
Residual forces of winner (n_{end})	0	2,626	0	2,646
Time in days to end of fight (t_{end})	18.1	18.1	18.1	18.1

a. Not available because Lanchester equations do not deal with movement.

In the analyses summarized in chapter 7, the ideal (or baseline) case assumed that all NATO forces were at full combat power and effectiveness, whereas the Warsaw Pact capabilities had been penalized, as appropriate, for the early use of cadre divisions with older sets of equipment, shortages of trucks, and reservists with little or no recent training. Since both sides consist of units with differing equipment, effectiveness, and nationality, both are treated as heterogeneous forces and penalized in performance to allow for the difficulty of coordinating their operations. Table C-5 summarizes the assumptions about the combat power and effectiveness of NATO and Warsaw Pact forces used to obtain the estimates of the enemy's relative lethality for the M + 120 contingency shown in chapter 7 (tables 7-4 and 7-7).

Let it be admitted, in conclusion, that theater-level conventional force planning is at best a relatively primitive art. Nonetheless, even in its present state, because assumptions are made explicit and causes and effects are clearly related, it remains preferable to static comparisons of various capabilities such as divisions, tanks, attack helicopters, and combat aircraft. It can also prove more useful than hunches and intuitions, no matter how professional their source. Improvements in existing models, or even new models that do not stray too far from the quantification of military experience and judgment, are certainly to be desired,

a contrasting view of the utility of the Lanchester approach, see Joshua M. Epstein, *The Calculus of Conventional War: Dynamic Analysis without Lanchester Theory* (Brookings, 1985).

Table C-5. Warsaw Pact and NATO Orders of Battle in the Attack Sector at M+120
Thousands of units of combat power unless otherwise specified

| | Baseline case | | Case 1 | Case 2 | Case 3 |
Item	Warsaw Pact[a]	NATO	NATO	NATO	NATO
Combat power					
Ground forces	3,434.10	1,679.5	1,559.5	1,439.5	1,439.5
Organic air defenses	343.41	84.0	78.0	72.0	72.0
Close air support	60.00	375.6	375.6	375.6	375.6
Total	3,837.51	2,139.1	2,013.1	1,887.1	1,887.1
Overall effectiveness	.0175	.0564	.0490	.0482	.0445
Index of NATO's lethality					
relative to the Warsaw Pact	.50	.50	.44	.40	.38

a. Warsaw Pact capabilities remain identical in all four cases.

as are continued simplicity and transparency. Equally important, explicitness about assumptions and greater clarity about the extent to which differences in those assumptions rather than differences in the models determine a particular outcome would help to advance the art. That analysts should try to advance the art rather than return to the drawing boards seems hardly in doubt.

INDEX

Abrams, Gen. Creighton W., 34–35
Academic and aptitude credentials of new recruits, 51n, 65–67, 69, 70
Active Component/Reserve Component Partnership Program, 80
Active Guard/Reserve (AGR) personnel, 6, 71–72
Affiliation Program, 80
Air Force Reserve, 1, 54, 99–100n
Air National Guard, 1, 54, 72, 99–100n
Allies' military responsibilities, proposed increase in, 134–36, 137
Army, U.S.: all-volunteer Army, conversion to, 27; attitude toward reserve forces, 39, 58–59, 62, 105–06; civilians, greater reliance on, 131, 137; command structure, reorganization of, 25; cost of maintaining Army battalions, 29–31; dependence on Navy and Air Force for deployment, 126; dependence on reserve forces under current force planning, 26–28, 36, 111–14, 127; equipment for reserve forces, 86–88; force reductions of *1970*s, 22–24; full-time reservists, resistance to, 72; funding shortfalls, 126; increase in active forces to reduce dependence on reserve forces, 130–32; readiness assistance for reserve forces, 25; training with reserve forces, 80
Army National Guard, U.S., 107; combat mission, 8; diversity within, 4; equipment for, 85, 86, 88; European war, deployment for, 13–14, 16–17; expenditures on, 17–18; force structure, 8, 9; growth of, 1; in Korean War, 41–42; manning of, 65–67, 68, 70, 71; membership, 5; payroll costs, 30; political influence of, 32; race and economic status of personnel, 51n;

readiness of, 93, 94, 95, 96; state control of, 5, 81; Total Army structure, place in, 10–12; training for, 102; in World War II, 38–41
Army Reserve, U.S.: CENTCOM forces, inclusion in, 16–17; diversity within, 4; equipment for, 85, 86, 88, 107; European war, deployment for, 14; expenditures on, 17–18; federal control of, 5; force structure, 9; growth of, 1; manning of, 65–67, 68, 70, 71; membership of, 5; payroll costs, 30; political influence of, 32; race and economic status of personnel, 51n; readiness of, 93, 94, 95, 96; support mission, 8; Total Army structure, place in, 10–12; training for, 102. *See also* Organized Reserve Corps
Army Science Board, 100
Army Training Board, 103

Bacevich, A. J., 106n
Baskir, Lawrence M., 51n
Bennett, Charles E., 33
Berlin Crisis of *1961*, record of reserve forces in, 20, 44–46, 61
Berman, Larry, 49n
Betaque, Norman E., Jr., 14n, 106n
Binkin, Martin, 23n, 32n, 33n, 42n, 51n, 66n, 67n, 68n
Blazing Trails training exercise, 82
Blechman, Barry M., 55n
Bodilly, Susan J., 30n
Boland, Herman, 42n, 43n, 44n, 46n, 57n
Bowman, William, 23n, 69n
Brewer, Garry D., 150n
Bright Star training exercise, 82
Brinkerhoff, John R., 69n
Brown, Harold, 133
Browning, James W., II, 16n, 108n